What people are saying about

Aos Sidhe

Our best short book on the Aos Sidhe: Morgan writes elegantly,
humbly and wittily about Ireland's oldest community.
Simon Young, folklorist

Pagan Portals - Aos Sidhe by Morgan Daimler is a well-researched
and timeless guide to understanding the Aos Sidhe, stripping
away the modern folklore of common parlance to find the rubies
and emeralds within. Daimler's respected research and voice
has borne fruit yet again. Sure to be referenced in future works
for years to come.
Amy Blackthorn, author of *Blackthorn's Botanical Magic* and
Blackthorn's Protection Magic

This handbook is essential for anyone looking to dip their toes
in the ocean that is Irish fairy lore and for those wanting to lay
the groundwork for their studies into genuine Irish fairy lore. It
is no easy feat to condense the vast corpus of Irish fairy lore into
a book of this size, but this treatise neatly ties the older material
into modern folk belief and serves as an excellent introductory
volume on the subject. This book also gives the reader the tools
to further their research and importantly differentiates between
good and bad sources pertaining to the subject.
Shane Broderick, folklorist

In her book *Pagon Portals - Aos Sidhe*, Morgan Daimler shares with
us magical lore as well as how to work with these enchanting
fairy beings. She also dispels many of the misconceptions of
these magical folk that have crept into our modern storytelling
so that we may have a more accurate idea of who the Aos Sidhe

really are. This wonderful book takes you into the liminal space between magick and history revealing the enchantment of the Aos Sidhe.
Chris Allaun, author of *Otherworld* and *A Guide of Spirits*

Once again, Morgan Daimler delights us with an exceedingly informative and useful guide to an aspect of Irish folk belief. This book is the perfect introduction to the Aos Sidhe, and guides the reader through many of the initial questions one might have when beginning to delve into this topic. As always, Daimler's writing is accessible and approachable, and this book will delight complete beginners to the subject of Celtic fairy lore, or those hoping to expand their knowledge. Daimler provides a wealth of knowledge within such a small book. I truly believe that this book will act as a leaping board for many who wish to delve into the world of the Aos Sidhe for years to come. Dispelling misconceptions, and tackling the most frequently asked questions, this book is a treat from beginning to end.
Mhara Starling, author of *Welsh Witchcraft: A Guide to the Spirits, Lore, and Magic of Wales*

Daimler has once again produced an invaluable resource. This book is for individuals who believe in, or want to believe in, the Fairy Folk and is an essential read for all of the above; a work that is intellectual, accessible, and absolutely un-put-downable. It was a literal cover-to-cover experience for me and I'm going to read it again as soon as I finish typing this sentence.
Courtney Weber, author of *Brigid: History, Mystery and Magick of the Celtic Goddess* and *The Morrigan: Celtic Goddess of Magick and Might*

An excellent overview of the Aos Sidhe and their place in Irish culture through time. The strength of Morgan's work is its sound foundation in the Irish source material which she clearly references and encourages and inspires the reader to dig deeper into this fascinating topic. This book is a great resource from someone who has researched the topic in depth and who seeks to ensure a strong introduction to help clarify what is from the original culture and belief and what are later add-ons. Another gem from an important author who can take the diverse and hard to find strands scattered through our medieval texts and present them in a concise, lucid and educational way. I consider Morgan a National Treasure of Ireland for her work in service to promoting indigenous Irish spirituality.

John-Paul Patton, author of *The Poet's Ogam* and *Lightning Bolts and Dew Drops: A Cauldron of Poesy*

Pagan Portals
Aos Sidhe

Meeting the Fairy Folk of Ireland

Pagan Portals

Aos Sidhe

Meeting the Fairy Folk of Ireland

Morgan Daimler

**MOON
BOOKS**

Winchester, UK
Washington, USA

JOHN HUNT PUBLISHING

First published by Moon Books, 2022
Moon Books is an imprint of John Hunt Publishing Ltd., No. 3 East Street, Alresford
Hampshire SO24 9EE, UK
office@jhpbooks.net
www.johnhuntpublishing.com
www.moon-books.net

For distributor details and how to order please visit the 'Ordering' section on our website.

Text copyright: Morgan Daimler 2021

ISBN: 978 1 78904 937 4
978 1 78904 938 1 (ebook)
Library of Congress Control Number: 2021942552

A CIP catalogue record for this book is available from the British Library.

Design: Matthew Greenfield

UK: Printed and bound by CPI Group (UK) Ltd, Croydon, CR0 4YY
Printed in North America by CPI GPS partners

We operate a distinctive and ethical publishing philosophy in
all areas of our business, from our global network of authors to
production and worldwide distribution.

Contents

For Aoibheall

With gratitude to UCD's National Folklore Collection, and their kind permission to use excerpts from the School's Collection in this work.

Author's Note

Every book ultimately reflects the biases of the author and for me this is not simply an objective topic but a reality that many people, myself included, experience. It also represents a vital aspect of Irish folklore that deserves to be recognized and appreciated in a world that tends to favour homogenization and fiction over older folk belief. I am not sure that any fair discussion of the Irish Aos Sidhe can be had without including the perspective of those who believe in these beings as tangible and real, nor should those views be ignored. This undoubtedly colours my opinions here but I have done my best to be objective in what is shared throughout this book. I want everyone, no matter what your viewpoints are, to find some value here.

I personally favour using APA citation in my writing and so throughout this book when a source is being cited you will see the name of the author and date of the book in parenthesis after that. Each chapter will also have end notes expanding on points that don't fit neatly into the larger text but are important to touch on.

Finally I want to say here that I am writing this book because of an aisling, a vision, I had and because I feel like this book is a necessary thing to help people sort out Irish folk belief from popculture and fiction. I am myself not Irish but rather Irish-American and I acknowledge that makes a difference in my own understanding and perspective but I have done my best in this work to look only at Irish material and Irish sources and to present the beliefs as objectively as possible.

Morgan Daimler, June 2021

Introduction

"Belief in fairies is one of the most widespread of all our folk-beliefs."
Jeanne Cooper Foster, Ulster Folk Beliefs, 1951, page 66

This subject is, truly, too immense to contain within a short introductory text such as this one, however, anyone interested in the subject must start somewhere. I hope that this humble text can offer a good beginning for those seeking to understand the Irish Aos Sidhe and the wider folk beliefs that surround them, which are layered and complex.

It's not uncommon in both early modern and modern texts written in English on this subject to use the word fairies for these beings, however, I will not do that in this book except where absolutely necessary. I am choosing to use the Irish terms and spellings in this text as much as possible because I believe that while the English equivalents can be useful in discussion, they can also create a false sense that those equivalents are much more similar than they actually are and perpetuate the ongoing erasure of the older beliefs in favour of newer views beings inserted in from outside cultures. The term fairy is used in Irish folklore but by people who generally have a different understanding of its meaning; for a wider audience who may have a stronger ingrained sense of fairies as small, winged sprites I hope that choosing to use the Irish terms will help clarify the profound differences. I am also going to use Irish spellings for terms and places as much as possible; the only slight variance from this will be the use of the older word sidhe rather than the modern sí, both because the older spelling is the more commonly used in many texts and may be more familiar to people and also because the modern word sí has several other meanings.

Aos Sidhe, and the related term Daoine Sidhe, means 'people of the fairy hills' or people of the Otherworld and this serves as a good general description of what they are. They are beings who interact with our world but exist in and come from a place that is foreign to our world, that is the realm of the sidhe, beneath the earth, also called an Saol Eile, the Otherworld. Sometimes the Aos Sidhe are also called simply the sidhe although that term also means the fairy hills in which they live.

Before we get into the bulk of this book, I think we must take a small space to quickly discuss the various qualities of source material and why some popular sources are problematic. It's an unfortunate fact that the most commonly recommended sources for Irish fairy folklore are also the ones that require the most discernment and may not accurately reflect actual Irish belief in these beings. Now we can certainly get into a philosophical discussion of whether or not beliefs born outside of Ireland but put into the context of Ireland or which are created by those outside the culture are still valid and still have meaning, but at the very least I think people need to be aware of what is a belief that is genuinely coming from Ireland and one that isn't, or one which reflects folk belief versus one that has its roots in a single person's creativity. Folklore is a fluid and shifting thing and it does change over time and reflect new ideas and influences, without a doubt, but nonetheless not everything labelled as Irish actually reflects Irish folk belief. WB Yeats, Esperanza Wilde, and Lady Gregory are popular Victorian era sources for Irish folklore but they are also sources which can be questionable (and should be questioned) and who often included material that can be found and verified nowhere else. As much as I like Yeats poetry, and I do, the blunt fact is his versions of Irish folklore are often more fiction than folklore, and so his material must be very carefully checked. The result of Yeats' popularity is a strain of fairy belief based largely or entirely on Yeats' works that do not in fact bare any resemblance to the actual folk beliefs they purport to reflect. In the same way many people are quick to recommend 'The Fairy Faith in Celtic Countries' as a premier source on fairylore but it must be understood in the context of its own time and taken with a grain of salt; while the anecdotal material is valuable the scholarly sections are largely useless and include many theories that have been debunked long ago.

The people who wrote and contributed to these books were not writing their own beliefs or recording their own stories. They were people of a higher social class, well educated, who may or may not speak the language of the people they were talking to, going into various areas as visitors or guests and then asking about these beliefs and stories. It's important when looking at any book to consider who is writing it and their place in relation to the culture or people they are writing about. You cannot read older Irish folklore collections without keeping in mind who wrote that material down; as much as we might like to see it as a natural snapshot of belief at the time it is more accurately understood as a posed portrait of the beliefs, filtered through the lens of the writers.

Why does this matter anyway? I think it's important to understand the various threads of folk belief out there. These Victorian era stories have been circulating for well over a hundred years and there are many people now who entirely believe them, despite their lack of historicity or deeper cultural veracity. There are also still extant beliefs about the same things these sources talk about which are entirely different in nature and description and that must be respected rather than argued against based on Victorian sources. I do think it's important to understand the variety and difference and to appreciate that these writings were more their own ideas than actual folk beliefs of the people at the time. That doesn't mean to entirely dismiss these versions, as I said they've been around now for over a hundred years and have a lot of modern belief behind them, but we must be clear that those popular versions aren't reflective of older or even necessarily modern Irish folk beliefs.

The best bet with this subject is to look to people who have grown up with these beliefs, people within the living culture, and people who have an established knowledge of the topic, such as in academia. Any information that seems new or contradictory to things within established belief should be cross checked, just to verify the source and whether or not it's an Irish belief from Ireland or a belief being labelled as Irish to give it an air of legitimacy. Because while there are a huge number of new beliefs germinated outside Ireland but labelled as Irish the folk beliefs within Irish culture are still there and the beings attached to these beliefs remain, as they always have, in that liminal space between consciousness and dream.

Chapter 1

Who Are the Aos Sidhe?

The story of the Aos sidhe stretches back to the beginning of written Irish myth and forward into the present, creating a complex set of beliefs and practices. None of these alone tells us who the Aos Sidhe are, but by looking across the totality of the material we can begin to form a picture of these beings.

In studying Irish folklore or talking to people you will find the word fairy used, as it is the closest English language equivalent to the Irish concept of the Aos Sidhe. You will also find a wide array of both Irish and English euphemisms that are used to refer to these beings. There is an ongoing debate about whether the word fairy offends the Good People or not and whether it is better to avoid using the word by sticking to other terms. The core idea behind this is that the Aos Sidhe can pass invisibly around humans and may be near without you realizing it and so will hear you speaking about them; if you use a term like fairies which they may not like they could respond badly. This same idea is also sometimes applied to the word sidhe. As Dáithí Ó hÓgáin explains it:

> *"Due to a combination of respect and fear, however, this word for them [sidhe] is usually avoided, and circumlocutions are used – such as na daoine maithe (the good people) and na daoine uaisle (the nobles). In ordinary speech, even those designations may not be used, and the members of the otherworld referred to simply as 'they' and 'them'. The common term for them in English is 'the fairies' but this term is also avoided in Irish folk speech."* (Ó hÓgáin, 1995, page 83)

Euphemisms may be favoured because of the idea that they

might remind the Good People that they can be good to humans if they choose to. The use of euphemisms for these beings goes far back and has been common for as long as we have written evidence of them. While many of these terms are descriptive, the general idea isn't that these are descriptive terms, necessarily, but rather, that they represent positive ways to speak about these beings which can remind them of their own potential to be benevolent, or at least not harmful. Throughout this book I will be using a variety of euphemisms for the Aos Sidhe and so am including a list here of both the historic and modern terms that you might find.

Aes Sidhe [people of the fairy mounds, modern Aos Sidhe] circa 7th-9th century Echtra Condla

Gáethshluagh [host of the wind] circa 13th century Accalam na Senórach

Túathgeinte [leftwards turning folk] circa 16th century O'Davoren's Glossary

Sidaige [dweller in a fairy mound] circa 16th century O'Davoren's Glossary

Daoine Sidhe [people of the fairy mounds]

Daoine Uaisle [Noble People]

Na hUaisle [the Gentry]

Na hUaisle bheaga [the little gentry]

Uaisle na gcnoc [gentry of the hill]

Daoine Maithe [Good People] in use by 19th century/early 20th, ref. Duchas.ie

Daoine Eile [Other People]

Slua Sí [fairy host] old or middle Irish *Sidshlúag*

An slua aerach [the host of the air]

An slua bheatha [the living host]

Slua bheatha na farraige [living host of the sea]

Slua sí an aeir [fairy host of the air]

Slua sí na spéire [fairy host of the sky]

Sióg [given as fairies, possibly sí + diminutive óg] probably 20th century[1]
Bunadh na gcnoc [people of the hills]
Cuid na gcnoc [part of the hills]
Dream na gcnoc [people of the hills]
An dream aerach [the people of the air]
An dream beag [the little people]
Lucht na mbearad dearg [people of the red caps]
An mhuintir bheag [the little family]
An bunadh beag [the little people]
Bunadh beag na farraige [little people of the sea]
Daoine beaga [the little people]

In English you will also see:

Othercrowd
Themselves
Good Folk
The People Outside Us

What Do They Look Like?

Yeats[2] described the Daoine Maithe as looking much like humans, although prone to wearing slightly outdated fashion. Described throughout accounts as around five feet tall, sometimes slightly taller, with a range of hair colours and body types, they may blend in with the humans around them if they choose to. We see the idea of their human appearance reinforced in much of the anecdotal evidence particularly stories of borrowed midwives, stolen brides, and musicians who spend a night inside a fairy hill, many of which describe interacting with beings that are about the size and appearance of humans, although distinctly not-human. There would seem to be then, at least one type of more powerful fairy people who do or can look very much like humans and may even pass for human to some degree; these are often referred to as the Daoine Uaisle, or the Gentry. Not all of the Good Folk fit these descriptions though and we also find those who are said to be between 18 inches and 3 feet tall and those who may appear in various animal forms. They may appear wearing any colour but most often are described in red or green, less often in white, or in some combination of these colours.

Where Are They From?

There are several different beliefs about where the Aos Sidhe came from and how they arrived in our world; these theories are often tied into how a particular person or group understands the nature of these beings. Below I will include several of the more popular theories that you will find, although you should understand that there is no one agreed on origin for these beings and in some cases, there are multiple versions of a particular theory which may not all be included here. And ultimately, it's quite likely that there is no one simple answer to this question, but many possibilities.

1 Gods. One of the main theories of the origin of the Aos Sidhe is that they were or are the Tuatha Dé Danann, the old gods of Ireland. We are told in myths that when humans arrived in Ireland, they fought with the Tuatha Dé Danann and eventually defeated them; part of the agreement of this defeat was that the humans would keep everything on the surface of Ireland while the Tuatha Dé would get the other half, that is the land below the surface. This story is told in more depth in two myths, De Gabail in t-Sida and Altram Tige Dá Medar. Once they had gone into the sidhe the Tuatha Dé Danann became members of the Aos Sidhe.

2 Angels. One of the most common origin stories for the Aos Sidhe within Christian cosmology is that they were angels who remained neutral in the war in Heaven. There are different versions of this belief but one common story is that when Satan rebelled against God and was defeated, God cast the angels who had fought with the Devil into Hell where they became demons and punished the angels who refused to take sides by casting them into purgatory or trapping them on earth where they became fairies. In another popular story it is said that in his anger over the rebellion, God threw open the doors of Heaven and all the angels were being pulled out; Michael begged God to relent and he finally shut the doors. Those angels who had fallen into the earth became demons while those who were still falling through the air became fairies.

3. Demons. Related to the second belief there is a less common belief that the Aos Sidhe are demons or otherwise under the authority of the Devil. In both of the above instances there is a strong thread of belief that the Good Folk are seeking salvation and several points of folklore rest on them asking a priest if they have any chance at Salvation. MacNeill relates a couple of these based on the idea that in older times the Aos Sidhe would work the fields during harvest time but when they asked a priest their question and were told that they had no chance for redemption, either because they lacked a soul or because they did too much evil, they refused to do any more work (MacNeill, 1962).

4. Fomorians. A primordial group of beings who appear as antagonists across Irish myth, there is at least one reference in the Cath Maige Tuired that explicitly calls the Fomorians the warriors of the sidhe. While this is not a particularly popular theory for the origin of these beings it is worth including here for consideration.

5. Primordial spirits. Of course it is always possible that the Aos Sidhe ultimately are none of the things that human mythology paints them as but rather are ancient spirits that pre-existed humanity. This origin is found in some anecdotal accounts and may be supported in myths which refer to the Riders of the Sidhe existing prior to the Tuatha Dé Danann going into the sidhe.

6. Humans. Although not the origin for all of the Aos Sidhe we do find stories of some of the people of the fairy hills having once been human. Sometimes the human is said to have died and is later seen among the fairy host while in other accounts the person is taken alive. Once taken they are transformed into one of the Aos Sidhe.

7. Ancestors. It has also been suggested, particularly in more recent years, that the Aos Sidhe may be ancestral spirits or the spirits of ancient humans. This theory does have some popularity to it especially among some pagans but is predicated on the idea that the sidhe (fairy hills) are Neolithic or bronze age burial mounds[3] and that the stories of the Aos Sidhe tied to these places represent an embedded memory of the original purpose of the places.

Beyond these more detailed and common views there are also many other personal ideas about the origin of the Aos Sidhe to be found in anecdotal accounts. 'The Fairy Faith in Celtic Countries', for example, includes testimony from various people across 19th century Ireland, some of whom believed the Good Folk were Fir Bolg (another mythic race) or were beings who came from the stars. There is no certainty to this subject, but many possibilities.

Where Are They?

While we can and do interact with the Aos Sidhe in the human world, as well as in dreams and visions, it's understood that these beings have a world or reality of their own as well. It's unclear in mythology exactly where the Aos Sidhe, or the Tuatha Dé Danann, came from but it is suggested that their place of origin wasn't the human world[4]. In one story of the arrival of the Tuatha Dé Danann in Ireland it claimed they arrived in clouds and mists and landed on a mountain, for example. Beyond this they are also understood to have a realm or existence beyond or outside the human world which we will discuss here.

The Otherworld – called an Saol Eile in Irish, the Otherworld is a complicated place, that may best be understood as a series of connected places rather than one contiguous location. Often in stories this is described as an island or series of islands off the coast of Ireland, which is generally hidden from mortal sight. These islands are unique to themselves but all have similar qualities in that they are outside the mortal world. The Otherworld may also be reached through the sidhe. The Otherworld has a different flow of time from the human world and is usually known for its lack of age or illness, although injury and death from conflict can occur.

The Sidhe – the fairy hills or Otherworldly hills are the other main location attributed to the Aos Sidhe although they shouldn't be understood as truly separate from or unique from the Otherworld, but more as gateways into it[5]. Just as the term Aos Sidhe itself is both specifically and generally applied there is a distinction and overlap between an Saol Eile and the sidhe. It's widely understood that the Aos Sidhe went into the sidhe after being defeated by the Gaels, although it is unclear in mythology whether they created the sidhe themselves or joined beings already there; both are hinted at in different stories. The stronger argument may, perhaps, be made for them joining existing beings within the sidhe although much depends on how the source is read. For example, we have this from the Mesca Ulad:

"Ireland was left to the division of Amorgen Glúnmár son of Mil, for he was a king's poet and a king's judge; Amorgen divided Ireland into two parts, giving the part under the ground to the Tuatha de Danann and the other part to the sons of Mil, his own people.

The Túatha de Danann went into the hills – the regions of the Sídhe – then, and they submitted to the Sídhe under the ground."

There is also a passage in the Altram Da Tige Medar that says that when they went into the sidhe the god Manannán had to teach them how to successfully live there, including giving them a means of special immortality and agelessness as well as showing them how to pass invisibly in the human world. He could do this because he was already a powerful force in the Otherworld, specifically the Otherworldly island of Emhain Abhlac.

The Good Folk do not exist within one cohesive grouping, for the most part, not only in how we understand them but also in how they interact with each other. There are very strong regional associations with specific groups of the Aos Sidhe who are usually under the leadership of a named king or queen; these groups do not always get along and there are many stories of contention between them, enough so that certain regions and Otherworldly kingdoms are known for their rivalries with each other. In some cases they fight actual battles, sometimes leaving white blood behind at the scene as proof of their battles, as their blood is believed to be white (Ó hÓgáin, 1995). In other cases they might engage in games of hurling instead of outright warfare, although it was taken just as seriously. These fights may occur to decide who gets the harvest of the other's land but often enough seem to occur for no explicable reason (MacNeill, 1962). There are stories of humans who witnessed these battles as well as many tales of a man who was drafted into the fight or the game so that it could move forward as it seems sometimes the

Good Folk cannot engage each other without the inclusion of a living mortal on the field.

Otherwise they live in much the same manner as their human neighbours, having livestock, tending crops, spinning[6], eating, drinking, seeking lovers, and enjoying entertainments. Like the humans around them they were even noted to enjoy smoking tobacco and drinking both whisky and poitín [poteen] (Ó Súilleabháin, 1967). There is at least one account I have heard of the Good Folk having a baptism for a baby within a sidhe, as we might expect humans to do. And yet despite all of these similarities they are also distinctly different from the humans around them: living across a wider time period, quick to react with extreme violence to things a human might find minor, seeming to delight in human suffering yet also sometimes inexplicably kind, and with a magical ability and knowledge that is beyond humanity. To begin understanding them is to hold these two opposing concepts in mind, that they are simultaneously very like humans and also very different from them.

End Notes

1. Per discussion with Shane Broderick and with thanks to him for pointing out many of the Irish terms. English translations, and any errors therewith, are my own.

2. Yeats is a popular but problematic source for folklore who was prone to creatively embellishing the material he recorded in ways that created new beliefs different from the existing folk beliefs. This is a common and pervasive problem with the Victorian folklorists.

3. It is true that some of the well-known sidhe are burial mounds or cairns, however, not all of them are and the story is no doubt much more complicated than this theory would imply.

4. Although I will note that some versions of the myth attempt to euhemerize the Tuatha Dé by offering both a mystical origin and then a pseudo-historical one that explains them as humans.

5. In most accounts its clear entering a sidhe means moving into a place that isn't of the human world, however, there are accounts that would seem to indicate the sidhe, in the sense of the place where the Aos Sidhe live, is literally built into the earth. For example, in one account of the Fairy king Finnbheara stealing a woman, her husband recovered her by digging into Finnbheara's sidhe and salting the earth.

6. There is a long and complex connection between the Good Folk and spinning which is too detailed to get into here. It is, however, worth noting the depth of the subject and its wider importance.

Chapter 2

Across Belief

It is true that we have no records from the pre-Christian Ireland to look at or draw from but the written records we do have, recorded by Christian scribes, go back well over a thousand years. The earliest account can be found in a myth called 'Echtra Condla' [Adventures of Connla] which dates in writing to the 9th century but is likely several hundred years older[1]. We also have a large amount of folklore as well as modern anecdotal accounts, showing that these beliefs and these beings both extend back into the earliest written history and extend forward to the modern day.

We will begin this chapter with a brief discussion of some of these sources and then look at various information we can glean from them, including times and places that are significant as well as powers these beings possess.

Mythology

We find the Good Folk mentioned across a variety of myths and stories, sometimes as major figures within the story and sometimes woven into the background. It would be impossible, given how often we see these beings appearing, to mention every single story in which they might occur but I do want to include a list of myths that are of particular note.

De Gabail in t-Sida – the Taking of the Sidhe. This story begins by relating how it is the Tuatha Dé Danann went into the sidhe after being defeated by the Milesians. As part of this story we find out that when they first retreated from the world above the humans had trouble; their cows wouldn't give milk and their crops wouldn't grow. An agreement is reached with the Dagda, king of the Tuatha Dé, that humans will give a tithe of their crops and milk to the Aos Sidhe and in turn the Aos Sidhe will ensure that the land and livestock flourish. This agreement between the Gods and humans is seen in later folklore between the Aos Sidhe and humans.

Altram Tige Dá Medar – The Fosterage of the House of Two Milk Pails. This story also relates the Tuatha Dé Danann being driven into the sidhe, and further, how the Tuatha Dé Danann learned to live among the sidhe. Specifically it relates how Manannán taught them to be immortal in this new world and to pass invisibly to humans by giving them the Féth Fiadha. The Féth Fiadha is given to the Tuatha Dé Danann by Manannán so that they *"could not be seen"* and he also teaches them *"to carry on their mansions in the manner of the people of the fair-sided Land of Promise and fair Emhain Ablach"* (Dobs, 1929). The story itself is more complex than what I am summarizing here but offers fascinating insight into older beliefs around the Good People and their relationships with and interactions with the human world.

Echtra Condla – The Adventures of Connla. The oldest story that includes mention of the Aos Sidhe, this story relates how the king's son, Connla is approached by a woman of the Aos Sidhe who wishes him to join her in her home which she describes as a great sidhe across the sea. This combines two beliefs we find in later folklore, that the Aos Sidhe live in the fairy hills and that the Otherworld exists or can be reached by crossing the sea. The fairy woman in this story is invisible to everyone but Connla but his companions hear him speaking to her.

Echtra Nera – the Adventures of Nera. One of the more famous adventure tales, this myth begins on Samhain when Ailill, king of Connacht, challenges any one of his people to go out into the darkness and place a rope around the ankle of a newly hung corpse. Nera takes up the challenge and goes out into the night where he finds the dead man who asks him for help and then later sees the host of the sidhe riding by and follows them into the sidhe of Cruachan.[2]

Echtra Fergusso meic Leiti and the Aided Fergusso meic Leiti – The Adventures of Fergus son of Leiti and the Death of Fergus son of Leiti. The first Irish appearance of Leprechauns – then called 'lucorpain' – are in the Adventures of Fergus, with further details about these beings appearing in Fergus's death-tale. In the first story we see the protagonist interacting with the Leprechauns who kidnap him while he sleeps; he awakens and fights them off, gaining a wish in exchange for their freedom. This story along with the related Aided Fergusso mac Leidi establishes Leprechauns as small people and also makes it clear that there are both men and women among them. This story also establishes a connection between the Leprechauns and water, as they both try to drag Fergus into the sea while he is sleeping and then, after he wakes up and captures several of them, agree to give him the power to travel under water without drowning. In the Aided Fergusso meic Leiti we see Fergus meeting the king of the Ulster Leprechauns, Iubhdán, and the queen Bé Bó after they journey to Emhain Macha and are captured. Although the Leprechauns cause Fergus great trouble trying to force him to free their king – stealing all the milk of the province, burning the mills, and blighting the corn – Fergus and Bé Bó would become lovers and Iubhdan would later give Fergus a wisdom poem that advised him on which trees to burn and which not to burn, as well as the associations of some of the trees.

Folklore

Stories of the Daoine Maithe appear across Irish folklore forming a huge body of material that can be drawn on to better understand these beings. While this folklore does exist within a

Christian cultural context it should be understood as something that is in a liminal state both within and transcendent of that worldview. You cannot separate the Catholic from the fairy faith in this material and yet at the same time the stories often reflect and describe things outside the purview of that religion. While some people do attempt to remove any clear Christian material from the folklore, I believe that to do so is not only to lose layers of richness and depth that are essential to understanding these beings but also to misunderstand who and what the Good People are. They have always existed in a symbiotic relationship to the humans around them, something we see reflected in their speech and clothing at the very least, and more than a thousand years of Christian culture has without a doubt had some effect[3].

I will note here again that it is important to understand that not all folkloric sources are created equal and it's important to use discernment rather than simply trust any source that claims to be sharing Irish folklore.

Anecdotal Accounts

A core resource to understanding the Irish fairy folk comes to us from anecdotal accounts, which exist across the last hundred years into today. These are personal accounts from individuals or small groups who have had an experience with the Aos Sidhe and have chosen to share it, or such accounts passed on from people who heard it from the original source. Anecdotal accounts are the core of what later becomes folklore and this material can't be under-rated. 'The Fairy Faith in Celtic Countries', while not an ideal source in many ways, does include valuable anecdotal material from the late 19th century. A more reliable source overall is UCD's folklore collection which represents a variety of folklore and anecdotes gathered in the early 20th century. A modern collection of anecdotal accounts and folklore can be found on YouTube where a gentleman by the name of Michael Fortune has gone to great efforts to record people telling stories they remember, including many relating to the Daoine Maithe; he also sells DVDs of these videos on his website.

Times & Places

There are certain times and places which are connected to the Aos Sidhe across folk belief. These often represent liminal points, the transition between one thing and another, such as the move from summer to winter or day to night.

31 October and the month of November are strongly associated with the Good Folk. During Samhain – which isn't really one day but a period of time – the Good Folk are known to be more active, especially the more dangerous sorts. The Slua Sidhe, or Fairy Host, rides the night and the Good Folk are thought to move from hill to hill, sometimes in grand processions. Because it's believed that the Daoine Maithe are moving at this time it is more dangerous to be out at night, to pass near rivers, and on the west sides of buildings, making extra caution a good idea around these areas. It's also a good idea to leave out a bit of something as an offering – perhaps milk or cream, or bread, or share a portion of your evening meal – to please any of Themselves who may pass nearby.

Samhain is also the time when any berries left in the wild are thought to become off limits to humans as they are seen after that point to belong to the Good Folk. In particular it is said that the Púca either urinates or spits on any berries remaining after Samhain, spoiling them for human use.

Bealtaine is another time period when it's thought that the Good Folk are more active and moving from hill to hill. For example, one belief was that on Bealtaine day it was wise not to lend out any milk, butter, or a coal from the fire, especially to a stranger, lest the person be one of the Good Folk in disguise and steal the family's luck for the year (Evans, 1957). A household's luck was intrinsically tied to the items which symbolized it – milk, butter, and fire – and to be tricked into giving any of these to dangerous powers like the Fair Folk was to voluntarily give them power over you; to do this particularly on Bealtaine when spirits of all kinds were abroad and their powers especially strong was the height of foolishness.

> *"Being associated with a ceann féile (chief festival), May Eve and May Day were supposed to be times of greater than usual activity among supernatural beings, Every lios ("fairy fort") in Ireland was said to be opened that night, and their inhabitants moved abroad in great numbers, often changing residence at that time."*
> Seán Ó Súilleabháin, 'Nósanna agus Piseoga na nGael'

As the quote above illustrates, just as at Samhain, every sídhe was believed to open and the inhabitants to travel out across the land. Bealtaine was also the time when babies and young brides were most likely to be taken and a person had to take great care when travelling, especially alone. Although today many people might think of Samhain as the most dangerous liminal time, in truth Bealtaine was equally dangerous and liminal. At other times of the year a person might still run the risk of running afoul of the Fair Folk – or if one was lucky and clever of earning their blessing – but at the turning points like Bealtaine every single one of my references all mention the ubiquitous presence of the Other Crowd, to the point that it was almost expected to see or experience something Otherworldly. To quote Danaher:

> *"Supernatural beings were more than usually active about May Day, and the appearance of a travelling band of fairies, of a mermaid, a púca or a headless coach might, indeed, cause unease or alarm but certainly would occasion no surprise, as such manifestations were only to be expected at this time."*
> (Danaher, 1972, p121)

There is a tradition of giving to the Daoine Eile on May Day. In the old days – and perhaps still in some places – it was traditional to make offerings on May Day morning of milk poured at the base of a fairy thorn or on the threshold of the house, and to take the cows to the sí and bleed them, with some of the blood tasted by the people and the rest given as an offering to the Daoine Uaisle (Evans, 1957). Any offering of food or drink, left on the doorstep of the house or at any known Fairy place, whether it's a lone fairy tree or fort, was also done and was thought to convey some protection on the person (Danaher, 1972). One might note that there is an important difference between being tricked into giving milk or butter without intent and giving the same things purposely as gifts; to be tricked is to lose your power but to give a gift freely is to show respect and hopefully create an amicable relationship; despite this there are some who will offer or give nothing from sundown on the last day of April until sundown on the first day of May.

Midsummer is another time that has strong associations with the Other Crowd, specifically 24th June. This day is connected to the Fairy Queen (and goddess) Áine as well as Manannán who was said to be a king of the Otherworldly island of Emhain Abhlac; both were given special acknowledgement on midsummer. The Daoine Maithe were especially active at this time of year and were known to be seen on the sídhe associated with them. Extra precautions were needed to stay safe from their mischief or outright maliciousness on this night.

Lughnasá is also a time connected to the Good People, when it's said that their activity influences crops. For example, in Limerick it was said that sometimes the Fair folk of Cnoc Firínne would fight their counterparts from Cnoc Áine through the medium of a hurling match, and whoever won would take the best of that year's harvest (MacNeill, 1962). As with the other times of heightened sióga activity the chances of a human being abducted by the Good Folk is higher now and various local folk tales relate these stories.

In Ulster folklore the Good Folk may be out and about on the full moon. Foster relates that it was a common motif in the stories of that area for a stolen woman to tell her human spouse that she could be rescued the next time the Good Folk were moving which was most often the full moon. Twilight and midnight are also common times noted in fairy encounters, although I'd mention here that dawn and the crowing of a rooster will drive a being of the Otherworld off.

Beyond specific times there are also places that are strongly associated with the Daoine Maithe. This includes not only the sidhe but also certain trees and stones as well as places that may not be visible to humans.

Sidhe – the fairy hills, also sometimes called a rath or lios, these are places that are so strongly associated with the Good Folk that the term sidhe means both Otherworldly hill as well as the beings who inhabit it. These locations can be found all across Ireland with specific local folklore attached to them. Sometimes these places are the remains of older Neolithic, bronze age, or iron age sites which became known later as places of the Aos Sidhe, sometimes they are natural formations or locations that were not shaped by human hands. Sid in Broga [Newgrange], Cnoc Meadha, and Ceathrú Chaol are examples of the former while Craig Liath, Cnoc Áine, and Brí Leith are examples of the latter.

Fairy Trees – a Crann Sidhe or fairy tree is one of the main things after the hill which is associated with the Daoine Sidhe. A lone hawthorn growing in a field is often considered a fairy tree and it is dangerous to bring harm to such a tree because to do so will invite the wrath of Themselves; it's also thought unlucky to bring a branch of the tree inside a home. It's an old custom to leave gifts for the Other Crowd at the base of a lone hawthorn (MacCoitir, 2003).

Stones and Wells – Less common than trees but there are connections between the Good People and specific stones or wells. In Killaloe there is a stone, called Crag Liath [grey stone] that is said to belong to the fairy queen Aoibheall and similarly in the same area there is supposed to be a well that is hers. As with the trees we see a great possessiveness over these places by the Good Folk, for example, in one story from Ireland a young man interfered with a well that was known to belong to the Fair Folk and in response they cursed it; when the man next went to drink from it, he fell in and drowned (Ballard, 1991).

Fairy Paths – it is believed that the Good Folk change their habitations regularly and also that they travel through the land for various other purposes when they choose to. They have their own special roads or paths that they use for this purpose which, like the Good Folk themselves, are invisible to human eyes. The main concern for humans with these paths is the accidental building of homes or barns on them, which always results in a negative response from the Daoine Maithe. If a person is lucky the worst result will be constant disturbances in the house as the Good Folk continue to follow their path, even through the new building. In the worst case though a person, their family, or their animals may die, or the family may suffer constant misfortune (Ó hÓgáin, 2006). It was a custom to set up stakes or other markers at the corners of where a house would be built and leave them over night to see if they were still standing in the morning. If they were then the house could be built, while if any had been knocked down it was seen as a sign that the house was one or partially obstructing a fairy path and needed to be moved.

All of these places have stories around them and all are seen as being the property of the Daoine Uaisle. To interfere with or damage that which belongs to them has terrible consequences, including potentially illness, madness, and death. There are several more famous accounts of the fate that befalls those who damage or destroy fairy places, especially trees, for example, it's said that the DeLorean car company failed because they cut down a fairy tree when building their plant at Dunmurry and suffered the consequences (Coulter, 2015).

Sidhe Gaoithe

The Sidhe Gaoithe, or fairy wind, is a phenomenon which occurs when the Good Folk are travelling invisibly around humans. It most often manifests as a whirlwind that appears inexplicably, for example, on a still day, and it's thought that it can cause illness or injury to humans it passes by. The malicious Slua Sidhe travels in whirlwinds, or on the wind more generally, and because of this the whirlwind is called the séideán sídhe [fairy blast] or sitheadh gaoithe [thrust of wind] (O hOgain, 1995; MacKillop, 1998).

Poc Sidhe

One of the most feared weapons of the fairies was the fairy stroke or poc sidhe, sometimes also called the fairy blast (see above). There are several modern Irish expressions associated with this term including 'poc aosán' which is a term for a sudden illness, 'poc mearaidh' meaning a touch of madness, and 'buaileadh poc air' meaning to be elfstruck or bewitched (O Donaill, 1977). Associated with the Slua Sí [fairy host] and the sí gaoithe [fairy wind] the fairy stroke was a sudden and otherwise inexplicable illness marked by a change in behavior and health. MacKillop suggests that this term is where we get the term stroke from for cerebral hemorrhages or aneurysms (MacKillop, 1996).

The fairy stroke could afflict both humans and animals but was differentiated from the similar elfshot in its symptoms and method of application. Unlike elfshot which used an arrowhead, sometimes invisible, to injure a person, fairy stroke was caused by a blow from the fairies themselves, or in rare cases being struck by a blunt object they threw. Fairy stroke might manifest as a sudden seizure or else a loss of mental acuity, which may be temporary or permanent (MacKillop, 1996). Getting the fairy stroke, like many things associated with the Good People could be a double-edged blade as it cost a person their health and mind but was also believed to convey a special esoteric knowledge (Wedin, 1998). There was also some crossover with changeling folklore as in some cases those who had received the fairy stroke were said to have actually been taken by the Good Folk while either a glamoured object or decrepit fairy was left behind instead (MacKillop, 1996). This is also true of those afflicted by elfshot indicating that both could be used either to torment people or as a means of taking those humans who the Aos Sidhe desired.

Those who were struck by the blast might simply be at the wrong place at the wrong time, may have transgressed an Otherworldly rule, or may have failed to adequately protect themselves. One anecdote tells of a woman struck by the fairy blast because she passed through a crossroads without carrying a bit of protective bread in her pocket while another man received the blast for trying to cut down a tree the Good People didn't want cut (Reiti, 1991). In other examples people were approached by Gentry who either offered them items or wanted them to do things and when the people refused, the Good Folk threw items at them; wherever the item struck the person was afflicted with pain, sometimes resulting in lifelong debility and other times in madness and eventual death (Reiti, 1991).

Fairy-shot

The ubiquitous weapon of the Daoine Maithe is fairy-shot or elfshot which caused a variety of maladies to its victims. The physical arrows do exist and are sometimes found – they are small Neolithic flint arrowheads but it's believed when used by the Gentry that they are invisible to humans. Finding such a small piece of flint or primitive arrowhead lying on the ground might lead a person to believe they had found a fairy-dart (O hOgain, 1995).

While some believed a found elf arrow should be thrown in water or buried lest it draw Otherworldly attentions, to others it was a powerful talisman, although it had to be kept covered from sunlight and not allowed to touch the ground again (Evans, 1957). To possess an elf-arrow was good luck and they had magical uses as well, being used in cures for sick cattle as well as herbal charms (Wilde, 1888; Evans, 1957).

When used as weapons by the Other Crowd elfshot was thought to be the cause of various pain and afflictions including a sudden seizure or paralysis, cramping, pain, bruising, wasting sicknesses, and even death (Briggs, 1976). The Daoine Maithe might use these arrows for anything from punishing someone for a minor offense, in which case the effect might be slight and temporary, to tormenting a person with great pain and suffering if they were truly angry. If they wanted to take a person, they might use elfshot to paralyze them then switch the person with a changeling or a glamoured item like a log (Briggs, 1976). If they wanted to take cattle a similar procedure was used, where the animal was shot and would waste away and die, thus going to the sidhe (O hOgain, 1995).

There were various cures for fairy-shot. One approach was to spill a bit of the cow's blood in a ceremony dedicating the animal to saint Martin (Evans, 1957). Often a specialist, a fairy doctor or bean feasa [wise woman], would be called in first to verify that a person or animal had been elfshot and if necessary to effect the cure (Jenkins, 1991). In some cases the effect of the shot was deemed permanent and could not be cured at all or the cure applied would not be strong enough to be effective. In some cases, similar to the cures for suspected changelings, the cure itself would prove fatal.

Ceol Sidhe

Fairy music may sometimes be heard by humans, often haunting them afterwards. If a person were in the area of a known Otherworldly residence or place associated with them, they might hear the strains of fairy music in the air as the Good Folk celebrated (Ó hÓgáin, 1995). By some accounts the famous musician Turlough O'Carolan learned his skill by hearing fairy music while sleeping next to or on the side of a sidhe. The Daoine Maithe were known to favour musicians and various stories tell of Themselves gifting musical skill or ability to humans, although such a gift often had a cost; many of the poets and musicians who were alleged to have gained from the Othercrowd lost their sight to the experience (Ó hÓgáin, 1995).

Invisibility & Physicality

It is generally understood in modern folklore that the Fair Folk cannot be seen unless they choose to be or unless a person has some special ability or power to see them. The idea of the Good People being able to go unseen by mortal eyes is well accepted but not necessarily well understood and can often lead to discussion of the related subject of whether or not they have physical forms. This seems to be rooted in the modern perception that we cannot see them because they are insubstantial or exist entirely as energetic beings, rather than that we cannot see them because they do not want us to see them. I would argue that they do indeed have physical forms, based on the amount of folklore in which they interact directly and substantially with people and the number of stories where children are produced. However, that issue aside we are left with an assumption that the Fair Folk can become, effectively, invisible as an idea that is embedded in folklore. I think it may be worth looking at how far back that idea stretches in order to appreciate how deeply rooted it actually is.

While the idea of fairies being invisible may seem to some readers a modern or new age concept in fact it goes back to the oldest written material we have on these beings. In the Echtra Condla the fairy woman who approaches Connla cannot be seen by anyone but him, and in the same way in an account from the Táin Bó Cuailgne Cu Chulainn and his charioteer Laeg see a man of the sidhe passing through the army that is opposing them unseen by all the other warriors. In the Tochmarc Etaine the rider of the sidhe who speaks a prophecy about Etain appears and seemingly disappears with no one the wiser as to where he came from or where he went afterwards. There are other similar stories in other texts, including the appearance of the fairy woman, Fidelm, in the Tain Bo Cuailnge. In the exact same way we find tales in later folklore and anecdotal accounts of people of the fairy hills who appear to specific humans but not others or who can choose who sees them in our world.

The second, related question, to address here is the physicality of the Daoine Maithe. Because they may pass invisibly and may be around humans even though the humans are unaware of them there is sometimes the idea that these beings are truly incorporeal. And we can find some support for that in stories of the Good Folk appearing and disappearing and seemingly passing through physical barriers. However, there are also very many stories where it's clear that these beings are physical and can interact with humans, whether those humans want to be interacted with or not. The bulk of evidence supports the Good Folk, at the least, having the ability to manifest physically if they choose to.

End Notes

1. Beveridge in her book 'Children Into Swans' suggest the date may go as early as the 5th century common era based on linguistic clues in the text. This is common with the Irish myths which often reflect oral material that existed before being preserved in writing.

2. Also known as Uaimh na gCat, the cave of cats, the sidhe of Cruachan is a well-known location strongly associated with the Morrigan.

3. On a cross cultural note we see something very similar with the middle eastern Jinn, who are intertwined with Islam and seem to have the same type of relationship with that religion that the Irish Daoine Sidhe have with Christianity.

Chapter 3

Changelings

One significant motif in folklore that I think we need to take a closer look at here is the beliefs around changelings. There is much modern confusion on the subject but also a significant amount of native Irish material to be considered. The concept of changelings also helps people better understand the Good folk and their complex relationship to humans.

A changeling as Dr. Jenny Butler says[1], is "*a fairy surreptitiously put in the place of a human being*". These fairy substitutes play a significant role in Irish belief, although one that is both sad and difficult to parse. In fairness to the subject an entire text could be written about changelings across folk belief, but I will do my best here to cover the subject as concisely as possible.

A changeling may be a member of the Good Folk or an inanimate object left in place of a stolen human; if a being of the Othercrowd it would either be a very old one seeking to be cared for or a fairy infant that was sickly and failing, while if an inanimate object it would most often be a stick or piece of wood magically made to appear as the human. These changelings would sometimes sicken and die, or appear to, while other times they would live in the care of the human family acting in ways very demanding and unpleasant. There is also a third, but much less common, description of a changeling as a possessed human who is being inhabited by the spirit of one of the Daoine Sidhe. A possible description of this third type can be seen here:

"*There is a certain amount of belief in "changelings" in this district though people are reticent about the subject. There is at present a woman living about a mile from my home, who is said to "have been in the fairies."*

It is said that when a tiny child, she got into a trance and remained so for years, neither talking nor eating, so it is understood that she was changed or "taken" by the Good People and kept with them for years. After some years she was returned and the changeling disappeared - and though quite normal and now married, this woman is always looked upon as having been "In the Fairies", but she is never regarded with any superstitious fear."
(The Schools' Collection, Volume 0888, Page 211)

While infants and young children are the most often thought of as potential changelings, indeed Katherine Briggs suggests they are the true definition of such beings, in Irish folklore we find a range of ages from infants through adults to which the term may be applied. The most common targets for abduction and substitution were infants, children up to about age ten, newly married adults, and new mothers; in some cases both an infant and mother might be taken while in others the infant would be left but the mother taken. One person related a story about a woman who died and shortly after, before the body had been buried, her husband was visited by one of the Good People who told him she wasn't dead but taken by the fairies; the husband then waited by the body with the door open and his wife came in to see her infant at which time he grabbed her (Evans-Wentz, 1911). After being restrained and struck with a charm he had prepared, the wife returned to her body, as the story was related, she revived and she went on to live a long mortal life (Evans-Wentz, 1911). In another tale with a less pleasant ending a bride died at her wedding, only to appear to her new husband later and tell him that she was actually among the fairies and that if he went to a certain place, he would see her passing by and could save her (Evans-Wentz, 1911). The husband went as she'd told him to but when he saw his bride among the passing Fairy Host, he found himself paralyzed and unable to move to grab her; he never saw her again after that, but refused to re-marry (Evans-Wentz, 1911).

There is no certainty as to why the Aos Sidhe take humans but based on the evidence we have from the various sources it seems that the primary reasons are: to increase their numbers, for entertainment, or simple whim. They take humans to increase their numbers either by transforming the human into one of their own or to use the human as breeding stock. Entertainment is another reason and this can range from people taken by a fairy monarch to join a feast, to storytellers or musicians, to those who are connected to something the Good Folk find amusing like horse racing. Those taken for entertainment, such as musicians, have the best chance of being released again within a reasonable time frame, while those taken for other purposes are generally not seen again unless they are rescued by another human and are usually the ones replaced by a changeling.

Signs of a changeling ranged a bit depending on which of the above substitutes was in play but generally could include a sudden change in temperament, failing health, constant hunger, a slowly altering appearance, failure to age, and (with the older sióg) a deceptive nature. There would usually be an incident or occurrence which precipitated or allowed the switch, most often when the child or adult was alone for an unexpected period of time without the proper protection against Otherworldly harm. For example, in one changeling account a woman left her baby under a tree to help with the harvest and returned to find he had been replaced, while in another account from the same source a woman left her infant in the care of an older child who failed to keep a bit of iron near the cradle allowing the baby to be taken. In another account from Ballycomoyle a group of boys went out picking nuts and one wandered off and fell asleep allowing a changeling to be sent back in his place (The Schools' Collection, Volume 0721, Page 072).

Protecting against abduction from the Aos Sidhe was an important aspect of folk belief and often hinged on either the use of iron or of Christian holy items. Iron would be placed near infants and children, for example, fire tongs, scissors, or nails; a modern application of this that I am familiar with is the pinning of a safety pin to a child's clothes. Baptism and holy water were also thought to be protective and ensure a person couldn't be taken, and sometimes this would be combined with iron by opening the scissors or placing the nails to form the shape of a cross.

Changeling folklore had a distinctly dark side centred on the recovery of stolen humans, and readers who are sensitive to discussions of abuse, torture, and murder should skip the rest of this section.

If a changeling was suspected, then usually a person knowledgeable about the Good Folk would be consulted; if confirmed the changeling would be forced out through various means to gain the return of the stolen human. Some of these methods, like going out to the local sidhe at a specific time and trying to grab the person back when they were spotted among the fairy throng or attempting to trick the sióg into revealing its nature, were generally harmless to the suspected changeling. Other methods were not, and these included threatening them with fire, threatening or burning them with red hot iron, holding them in running water, dousing them in urine, leaving them out on manure piles overnight, or forcing them to consume herbal concoctions. The idea was that if the changeling revealed themselves, they would have to leave or if they were mistreated then the Good Folk would come to take back their own and would perforce have to return the human they had taken. This of course resulted in some horrific cases of child abuse, domestic abuse, torture, and murder. We will look at four examples here.

The Case of Thomas Leahy – 1826 – A 4-year-old boy, Thomas was paralyzed and mute. Judged a changeling he was 'washed' in the river Flesk for three consecutive mornings, but on the third morning was held under too long and drowned. The women who did this were charged but found not guilty of murder, as the judge felt they had not acted with the intent to kill him. (Crofton, 1828)

The Case of An Unnamed 6-year-old boy – mid-19th century – The child was reported to have had smallpox and recovered, but was not as healthy as he had been before falling ill. The child's father was staying at a lodging house and the woman running it suggested the boy was a changeling left for the real child and blamed him for her own bad luck. According to the child's aunt the woman told the father that he should behead the boy and put the head behind the fire to get the real child returned. The child was subsequently murdered and the father imprisoned for his death. (Young, 2011)

The Case of Mary Anne Kelly – 1862 – 5-year-old girl Mary was described as having *"softening of the brain and partial paralysis"* quite likely from an aneurism or stroke in infancy. Treated by a fairy doctor as a changeling the girl was given foxglove potions, stripped, and carried out on an iron shovel to be left on the refuse heap. The child subsequently died. (Young, 2011)

The case of Bridget Cleary – 1895 – Perhaps the most well-known of all changeling cases in Ireland was the 1895 death of Bridget Cleary. 26-year-old Bridget Boland, later Bridget Cleary, was married but was a very independent woman who had chickens, sold eggs, had a sewing machine and was a trained dress maker. Her husband Michael Cleary was a cooper. Bridget became ill in early 1895, after running an errand to a family member's home, with what was diagnosed as bronchitis by a doctor. Her husband and family became convinced she was a changeling, possibly in part because they lived so near a sidhe and Bridget had been past it before falling ill. At the urging of a local fairy doctor she was given a 'cure' or treatment for being a changeling which included being force-fed herbs soaked in milk, having urine poured over her and chicken dung put on her, and being jabbed with a red-hot fire poker. She was fed a piece of buttered bread, by one account, while being asked three times if she truly was Bridget Boland – when she wasn't able to answer the third time she was held over the fire. This went on for several days with various family members going in and out of the home. Finally she was doused in lamp oil and set on fire; her body was buried in a shallow grave. Her husband and several family members would later be charged and convicted in her death.

As grim as these stories are it is important to understand this aspect of changeling belief in order to get the full picture of the folklore. Many of the accounts in the School's Collection speak of babies, children, and adults who were safely recovered and went on to live ordinary lives, a hope which fed the darker side of the beliefs.

Changeling folklore is complex, and while folklorists and historians have offered a variety of possible explanations[2] for the belief it should be noted that the people who shared these stories and acted on them did truly believe in changelings as fairy substitutes for a stolen human being.

End Notes

1. Quoting from Dr. Butler's 2021 Myth and Magic: An Introduction to Irish Folklore course offered through University College Cork.

2. These are usually focused on infants and toddlers alleged to be changelings and look for physical disorders or behavioural issues that might explain the descriptions of the changeling. This is of course coming from the perspective that the Good Folk do not exist in any sense and so belief in them is base superstition and a misunderstanding of natural occurrences.

Chapter 4

Types of Fair Folk

Although they are often referred to simply as Aos Sidhe or one of the other euphemisms mentioned at the beginning of this book there are also many specific types of Otherworldly beings that we find mentioned in folklore. In this section we will discuss some of those particular types, although the reader should understand that whether or not these beings are considered Aos Sidhe may be murky or unclear and opinions vary. In some sources all of these beings are lumped together as People of the Fairy Hills while in others there is a clear separation and yet other places separate some but lump together others. I am presenting them all here with a short description of the related beliefs about them and the reader may decide which ones best fit the wider description of Aos Sidhe.

Some readers may notice there are names missing that they might have expected to be included. Of course I may omit some through error, as I am as fallible as anyone else, but generally I am doing my best here to include Irish Otherworldly beings that I can actually verify in folklore and belief. This means that pseudo-Irish beings like the Bean Tighe, which was created in the late 20th century outside Irish culture, will not be mentioned here. My hope is that this will help give readers a sense of what is and what is not actually a being from Irish folklore.

Alp Luachra
Found in both Irish and Scottish folklore the Alp Luachra is a being that inhabits a human body and consumes any food the person eats. The name is usually explained as 'fierce little creature' although the Irish is obscure; Alp means devourer or to swallow whole but Luachra is harder to pin down. Douglas

Hyde includes a stereotypical story of this being in his book 'Beside the Fire' where he tells a tale of a man who develops a mysterious wasting sickness only to finally be diagnosed with an Alp Luachra. He had fallen asleep next to a small stream and the creature had crawled into his mouth; inhabiting his body it was consuming his food so that he wasted away. The only cure according to Hyde's story was to eat a great deal of salty food and then go lie near a body of water so that the Alp Luachra, maddened by thirst, would be forced to leave.

This supernatural creature has a very earthly origin, however, in the common newt (Triturus Vulgaris) which is known as the Mancreeper or Manleaper, likely because of the stories of Alp Luachra (Colton, 2016). In folklore related to the newt, by the name of Alp Luachra, The Schools' Collection, Volume 0614, Page 321 discusses a cure for burns which is obtained by licking the Alp Luachra; the person who did so[1] would have the ability to heal burns afterwards.

Aos Sidhe

By definition the people of the Fairy Hills, the Aos Sidhe, are both a more specific group made up of human like beings said to be part of or descended from the Tuatha Dé Danann as well as a more general term for Otherworldly beings. In Irish mythology there are references to beings within the sidhe [fairy hills] before the Tuatha Dé went into them hinting that while the Tuatha Dé may be part of the Aos Sidhe they are not the totality of the Aos Sidhe. Who or what the beings that predated them are is unclear but we do have descriptions of various beings from the Otherworld that do not seem to be human.

Amadan na Bruidhne

The Fool of the Fairy Hill. Popularized by Yeats this being is obscure in folk belief but can be found, although the bulk of material about him is clearly drawn from Yeats' descriptions. He is said to wander in June and if he sets his sights on a human and touches them, he can drive them mad, cause paralysis, or even kill them (MacKillop, 1998). His appearance is unclear, with descriptions ranging from a young man with distorted features to an animal (Yeats, 1962).

Bean Sidhe

Perhaps the most well-known of Irish Otherworldly beings is the Bean Sidhe [plural mná sidhe], who is widely understood to be a death messenger or omen. The term Bean Sidhe literally means 'woman of the fairy hills' or 'woman of the Otherworld'. While the term does sometimes appear in a literal sense in older material it is most often used now to signify a specific type of being who is attached to a particular family or family line and who appears to weep and cry when someone in the family is about to die. It is commonly believed that the only people who will hear a Bean Sidhe are those within the family she belongs to (Ballard, 1991). In one 19th century account from Lough Gur, two women heard the Bean Sidhe when their sister was dying (Evans-Wentz, 1911). There are a few stories, though, where anyone in the immediate area heard the Bean Sidhe wailing and crying before a death, whether they were related to the dying person or not. The cry of the Bean Sidhe may sound like a screaming fox, howling dog, or moaning human scream, as well as the more common sound of a woman keening.

As with the Aos Sidhe themselves when we look at who and what the Bean sidhe may be, we do not find definitive answers but instead a multitude of theories across folk belief. It is likely that there is no single answer here but that what the Bean Sidhe is may be one of many different options. One possibility is that a Bean Sidhe is the spirit of a woman who was murdered while pregnant or died during childbirth (MacKillop, 1998). Tragic deaths are also given as a reason for the Bean Sidhe in other theories, including that she is the spirit of an unbaptized child, the ghost of a woman killed by a family member, or the ghost of a woman who lost her family and is still mourning them (Lysaght, 1986). Other folk belief places the Bean Sidhe as the spirit of a human who was a keening woman[2] in life but failed in her duties and so is trapped in a kind of purgatory now where she must continue to cry for the dead, or of an especially proud woman who is similarly being punished (Lysaght, 1986). As with other fairy origins there are also theories that the Bean Sidhe might be a fallen angel, a fairy, or even the child of a fairy and a human; Lysaght in her excellent book 'The Banshee: The Irish Death Messenger' discusses all of these ideas in depth. Finally the Bean Sidhe is connected to the Tuatha Dé Danann through several members of the Tuatha Dé who are also known as Mná Sidhe [banshees] including Clíodhna, Aoibheall, and Áine. These fairy women were known to have human lovers and to have children in human family lines, giving them motivation to follow those family lines and mourn over deaths within them. The Bean Sidhe is also associated with the war goddess Badb and in some areas of Ireland the word badb (pronounced in those dialects as bow[3]) is the name used for the Bean Sídhe; like Badb the Bean Sí is able to take the form of a hooded crow (MacKillop, 1998).

Descriptions of the Bean Sidhe vary but in general she is described as beautiful. She is often described as a grey figure or a woman wrapped in a grey cloak, although by other accounts she wears a long grey cloak over a green dress with her eyes deep red from crying (Ballard, 1991; Briggs,1976). Others say that the Bean Sídhe wears white, or white with red shoes, and has long golden hair (MacKillop, 1998; Logan, 1981). She brushes her hair with a special comb and it is considered very dangerous even today to pick up a stray comb you find laying on the ground, in case it belongs to this spirit. Folklore tells of those who find a silver or gold comb and bring it home only to be confronted at night by horrible wailing and scratching at the windows until they pass the comb out on a pair of tongs which is pulled back in twisted and broken (O hOgain, 2006). We have an account of such an event here:

"Once there was a crowd of boys coming home from a local dance and they were boasting about the great things they could do, one of them more than the others. They saw the bean-sidhe combing her hair, and the others said to this boy "Would you take the comb off the bean-sidhe". So he went over and he took the comb off her. The next night they were sitting around the fire and the bean-sidhe came to the window and asked for her comb. The boy put the comb on the top of the tongs and put it out through the window to her. She took the comb and broke the tongs to bits and she said "If it was your hand I would have done the same to it". The next morning all his teeth were gone."
(The School's Collection, Volume 0568, Page 298)

Although sometimes assumed to be the cause of death in folklore, the Bean Sidhe is clearly an omen or messenger of death and not its cause.

Cat Sidhe
Stories of cait sidhe – fairy cats – are primarily found in Scotland, however, there are some few modern references to them in Ireland. Described as dog-sized black cats with a spot of white on their chest they are associated with the wider folklore about the King of Cats and often seen as a bad omen.

Clúracán
Often used interchangeably with the word Leprechaun; there is little distinct folklore about this being. Ó hÓgáin suggests the name is a simply a corruption of the more well-known Leprechaun and that the two beings are identical.

Cú Sidhe

Fairy Hounds. In Irish folklore Cú Sidhe may be hounds that belong to the Aos Sidhe and who are used to guard treasure, especially gold, or may otherwise be fairy hounds which similarly guard locations. There are a few accounts in the School's Collection of cú sidhe guarding gold, although it isn't always treasure of the Tuatha Dé Danann and may sometimes be human treasure that has been hidden in ruins. For example, in one story which was recorded in Irish[4] we are told:

> *"It is said that a pot of gold is hidden in the old temple in Maghruis cemetery. It was said that anyone who found the gold would lose a piece of his finger, because a hound of the sidhe was guarding the pot.... a man came once and decided to go find the gold whatever it cost. He was soon chasing and digging through the brambles and came to a large broad slab. He thought of raising it but heard a noise behind it. He thought it was the fairy hound..."*
> (The Schools' Collection, Volume 0010, Page 003)

In at least one Irish example a small white fairy dog appeared as an omen of the coming of the Daoine Sidhe to a home, to warn the inhabitants to prepare (Evans Wentz, 1911).

Dobharchú

Translated as otter but literally meaning 'water dog' the Dobharchú appears in older stories as a monstrous creature that looks like a hound but lives in the water, often causing harm to humans or animals nearby. It takes the role in some folk stories of the inexplicable monster that appears without warning and is difficult to hunt down. In 2016 I was told a story of a Dobharchú by a man in Sligo, who related that the creature dragged a woman to her death in the river and was then pursued to Cnocnarea by her grieving husband and one of his friends; after finally being run to ground it was killed but not before it killed the horses that the men had been riding.

Dullahan

A spirit that may be either a ghost or fairy and which appears headless, riding a horse. In most accounts the Dullahan is mounted but there are some that place him in a coach instead and variations where the horse or horses are also headless (MacKillop, 1998). The horse (or horses) are said to be black with red eyes and the Dullahan carries his own head, and some say he also carries a whip made of a human spine. Those who hear him passing and dare to look at him may be blinded by his whip and anyone who dares open their door as he goes by will be drenched in blood (MacKillop, 1998).

The name is uncertain; MacKillop suggests it may come from 'dubh-luchrachan' meaning dark, puny creature but I personally favour 'dubh laochan' meaning dark warrior.

Each Uisce

Each Uisce literally means water horse and that describes them quite effectively. They are Otherworldly beings who appear in the form of beautiful horses, who live in bodies of water – especially lakes – and may go on land if they choose to. Danaher claims that Each Uisce are the most common of the water monsters found in Irish folklore, asserting that stories of them are attached to almost every body of fresh water. Each Uisce are known to appear on land as a beautiful tempting horse but once a rider mounts, they find themselves unable to let go of the animal and are immediately taken into the water, drowned, and eaten. Some Irish folklore also tells of Each Uisce luring horses into the water and drowning them as well.

In one anecdotal account a man was riding near a lake in the evening when a water horse rose from the water and cried out, causing the horse the man was riding to plunge into the lake; the man escaped but the horse was never seen alive again (The

School's Collection, v 1047, p 24). In another account a man in Sligo was in need of a horse to plow with and saw several water horses by the side of Loughnaleva. He caught one and hitched it to his plow safely enough but when he later tried to ride it, the water horse ran with him back into the lake where he was killed by the group (The School's Collection, v 380, p 356-357)

Fear Dearg

Meaning 'Red Man' the Fear Dearg, as his name implies, appeared dressed in red with a red hat. His appearance otherwise varied greatly depending on the source, with everything from a giant to a human sized figure to a 2 foot tall being described (Briggs, 1976). The longest descriptions of him come from Yeats and Croker[5] who say that the Fear Dearg was a trickster; Yeats paints him as malicious while Croker compares him to the English Puck, mischievous but not truly dangerous.

Geancánach

The name probably means 'love talker', although the entry in the Irish Dictionary will give you 'fairy cobbler', playing on the folk connection between these beings and leprechauns. The Geancánach is most well-known from Yeats' writing, where he is characterized in 'Fairy and Folktales of the Irish Peasantry' as a solitary being who haunts lonely places smoking his pipe and seducing women who then fade away and die, apparently having lost the will to live. Yeats' account, which was said to be quoting a direct source, claimed that the Geancánach was *"of the same tribe as the leprechaun"* but unlike the leprechaun was the embodiment of *"love and idleness"*. This idea of the Geancánach as a seductive and dangerous solitary being has become common, even finding print in Katherine Briggs' book 'A Dictionary of Fairies'.

What we find in accounts from Irish folklore, however, are a very different being. In these accounts the Geancánach is described synonymously with the Leprechaun, wearing red and green, smoking a clay pipe, and offering gold or wishes to those who capture him; the term is also used interchangeably with the English word fairy. They have no inherent connection to seduction or the deaths of women, and the dictionary definition of the word to this day, as mentioned, means a 'fairy cobbler'.

These are typical descriptions of this being from The School's Collection:

"It had a red cap with tassel, a red jacket, green breeches and stockings and leather shoes. It was 2' 6" high."
(the School's Collection, vol 0978, page 124)

"The Geancánach another form of Leprechaun appears with his hands in his pockets and a duidin [clay pipe] in his mouth. It meant marriage for a girl to meet him ill luck for a man."
(the School's Collection, vol 0491, page 304)

Grogach

A type of being known in Ulster, imported from Scottish folk belief, the Grogach is a human-like being that prefers wild places or farms and may help with cattle. The name is related to the older Irish word for hairy and these beings, male and female, were known to wear nothing but their own hair, preferring nudity. In one account relayed by Briggs a Grogach is driven off by a gift of clothes which offends him and convinces him the family he is connected to wants to be rid of him.

Leannán Sidhe

Leannán sidhe literally means 'Otherworldly lover' referring to one of the aos sidhe that takes a human lover. Yeats wrote about this being in his 1888 'Fairy and Folktales of the Irish Peasantry' where he said this:

"The Leanhaun Shee (fairy mistress) seeks the love of mortals. If

they refuse, she must be their slave; if they consent, they are hers, and can only escape by finding another to take their place. The fairy lives on their life, and they waste away. Death is no escape from her. She is the Gaelic muse, for she gives inspiration to those she persecutes. The Gaelic poets die young, for she is restless, and will not let them remain long on earth—this malignant phantom."

This short description has formed the foundation for the wider modern understanding of this being and is how many people conceptualize them.

The problem is, Yeats' characterization is almost entirely his own ideas of the poet's dark muse, popular at the time he was writing, rather than any native Irish idea of what a Leannán Sidhe was. His clear gendering of the being as female is one sign of this, as the term leannán isn't and has never been applied only to women. In point of fact the term can be found going back about a thousand years or so used for any of the aos sidhe who took a human lover without any inherent negative connotations – one example is Aoibheall, a queen of the people of the sidhe in Munster. Aoibheall is seen as the protector of the Ó'Brien clan because it is said in stories that she was either the lover of king Brian Boru or possibly his son Murchadh. Gearóid Ó Crualaoich in his 'Book of the Cailleach' relates a more recent example of a leannán sidhe (male) who was seen gathering herbs with a bean feasa [wise woman] on several occasions. MacNeill also discusses several Leannán Sidhe, connecting them to figures in mythology and to fairy woman who acted as guardians of family lines. Ó Súilleabháin relates a story about a leannán sidhe associated with Inchin Castle who eventually left her human lover when he broke a geis [taboo] she had set on him not to invite others to the castle. The idea of a human losing their leannán sidhe through such means is seen in other stories as well, often leaving the human to pine for the lost Otherworldly lover.

We can find both concepts of the leannán sidhe in current

belief, as illustrated by the definition of leannán in the Foclóir Gaeilge-Béarla which encompasses both the straightforward 'fairy lover' (1 e, i) as well as a 'baleful influence' (e, ii) and 'a chronic sickness' (2) (Ó Dónaill, 1977).

Leprechaun[6]

The name Leprechaun appears under various versions and spellings as far back as 1600 in English and the 8th century in Irish. The etymology of the name is uncertain, with the leading theory previously was that it came from the Old Irish lúchorpan meaning a 'very small body' (Harper, 2017). This idea is based in the word breaking down to 'lú' meaning something small + corp, a body (a loan word from Latin) + an, a diminutive ending indicating again something small. In the electronic 'Dictionary of the Irish Language' lúchorpan is defined as *"a dwarf or water-sprite"* and connected to a possible Latin root[7] (eDIL, 2021). There is also a very popular folk etymology that says the word comes from leith-bhrogan meaning one shoe maker, however, this probably doesn't go back further than the 19th or 18th century.

An aspect of uncertainty with Leprechauns is whether they belong among the ranks of the Aos Sidhe or are a separate and distinct type of being. In the older folklore and mythology it is plain that the Leprechauns are their own group of people, distinct in both appearance and powers from the Daoine Sidhe. However, in later folklore the word was often used as a generic term indicating all small fairies, and conflated with the other beings including the Aos Sidhe who had by then been diminished. They were also explicitly tied in folk belief to the God Lugh and by extension to the Tuatha Dé Danann. This later folk connection muddies the waters when trying to categorize these beings, so for our purposes here they will be included along with other distinctly named beings.

The first appearance of Leprechauns – then called 'lúcorpain' – is in the Echtra Fergusso Meic Leiti. The Leprechauns of this millennia old story are very different from the ones we find in modern folklore and popculture, except for their size. They are a kind of water sprite with control over crops and livestock and live in their one kingdom.

Descriptions of Leprechauns generally agree that they are small, as their name implies. A poem by William Allingham describes a Leprechaun as *"a span and a quarter in height"* or in other words 30 centimeters or 12 inches (Allingham, 1888). The Echtra Fergusso meic Leiti describes them as about three *"fists"* high, which one might estimate to be about the same size. The mythology describes a range of appearances and genders, saying that king Iubhdán's bard had fair hair while the king himself was dark haired, and that queen Bé Bó was beautiful enough that Fergus desired her despite her tiny size. Later folklore, however, tends to describe Leprechauns as exclusively male, old, grey or white bearded and sometimes wearing glasses (Briggs, 1972).

Allingham says the Leprechaun was plainly dressed in drab clothes, wearing an apron and with buckles on his shoes; he is sometimes described wearing a red hat as well (Briggs, 1972). In contrast Lady Wilde prefers to describe them as cheerfully dressed in green, however, this view cannot be traced back before her as far as I have been able to find. There is a good amount of 19th century folklore that describes Leprechauns wearing red, sometimes exclusively. This may represent legitimate folk belief, as red is a color strongly associated with the Otherworld and red hats or shoes in particular are a common item for them to be described wearing. There has been some suggestion, however, that the descriptions of Leprechauns wearing only red is the result of one folklorist writing in the early 19th century so there is some uncertainty here.

In modern folklore the Leprechaun is a shoe-maker, always seen working on a single shoe. I have heard people say that the fairy has a malicious side and that he will try to trick a person into trying on the shoe, after which they will be unable to remove it and compelled to dance until they die[8]. The Leprechaun is believed to have great hordes of treasure as well as the ability to grant three wishes to anyone who captures him, but he is notoriously difficult to trap as he is very clever. In many stories a person may think they have gotten a Leprechaun only to take their eyes off of him for an instant and find he has disappeared. In some stories he blows the tobacco from his pipe or snuff into their faces in order to make them sneeze and have time to escape, Leprechauns being said to enjoy smoking pipes when they aren't cobbling shoes. In other stories he will divulge the location of his treasure which the person will mark with a handkerchief or rag only to return and find the entire area covered in identical markers.

Older folklore, via the mythology, showed us a complicated society which included monarchy, poets, bondwomen, and everything else we'd expect in Irish society at that time; basically the Leprechauns of 8th century Ireland had a society that mimicked or mirrored Irish society itself. The King of the Leprechauns was put under geasa [taboos] by his poet which led to the situation in which he was captured by Fergus, for example. Yet modern folklore tells us that Leprechauns are solitary shoe-makers who amass great treasure that can only be gained if they are captured and tricked into turning it over. Both views grant the Leprechaun power, but the newer view has lost the connection to water and sociability, while the older view lacked the hidden treasure and don't-look-away-or-he'll-be-gone idea.

One can see the disconnect between older folklore and newer in the views about whether a Leprechaun is solitary or social. The mythology paints a picture of social beings who live in a monarchy and were willing to fight to get their king back when he was captured by a human king. Yet renowned modern folklorist Katherine Briggs tells us that leprechauns are solitary fairies and when seen appear alone (Briggs, 1972). Yeats also supported the idea of Leprechauns as solitary fairies, as did many of the writers of his time, although this may be drawing heavily from a single

Irish-American source, McNally's 'Irish Wonders', which lays out a great deal of Leprechaun lore that was simply repeated by other folklorists afterwards. The difficulty of course is that this written folklore has taken root and become the widespread modern lore of the last century and a half, which many people have believed is all of the Leprechaun story.

When we look at the folklore of Leprechauns, we are presented with two very different pictures. The oldest mythology shows beings who are social, hierarchical, connected to water, and distinct from the Daoine Sidhe. Modern folklore describes almost entirely different beings: solitary, male, earthy, and conflated with the Daoine Sidhe. In some cases we can surmise where a tidbit of folklore came from, for example, the idea that capturing a Leprechaun would give a person three wishes is most likely a confusion of Fergus's story where he captured three Leprechauns trying to take him into the sea and agreed to spare their lives in exchange for a wish. In other cases, such as the idea of Leprechauns as fairy shoemakers, we are left with supposition that perhaps its rooted in the folk etymology of the name. Powerful society of diminutive water spirits or solitary earthly shoe-makers, both versions of the Leprechaun can be found in folklore.

Maighdeana Mhara

Literally 'sea maidens' although it's often translated as mermaids. Like the Bean Sidhe the Maighdean Mhara (singular, sea maiden) is known to be fond of combing her hair with a gold comb and may be seen with a mirror. Unlike classical mermaids the Irish Maighdean Mhara may be found in the sea or in fresh water lakes; she is associated with the salmon and some stories give her a salmon's tale. The most famous example of such a being may be Li Ban, a woman mentioned in the 16th century 'Annals of the Four Masters' as a pseudo-historical woman who survived the overflowing of a holy spring within an underwater cave. After a year trapped there, she prayed to leave and was transformed into a salmon below the waist. She lived that way for 300 years in Lough Neath before being baptized as a Christian and dying.

Murúcha

A type of being comparable to the mermaid, which is what the Irish is given as in English. The folklore is similar to the Maighdean Mhara but a Murúch can be male or female, with the females renowned for their beauty and the males for their ugliness, and Murúcha are said to have webbed hands. Murúcha have a red-feathered hat that allows them to shapeshift and come onto land in the form of a hornless cow, but if the hat is lost then they will be trapped there (Briggs, 1976). These beings sometimes take human lovers and may produce children with them which are notable for having a few scales.

Púca

In old Irish púca is given as 'a goblin, sprite' and similarly the modern Irish is given as hobgoblin (eDIL, n.d.; O Donaill, 1977). These translations give a clue to the Púca's nature, which may be described as mischievous but can in folklore be either helpful or harmful. In some sources the Púca was seen as purely evil and dangerous, while others described it as potentially helpful and willing to do work around the home if treated well (McKillop, 1998). This is also another being which occupies a liminal place, being seen as both one of the Good Folk and also possibly a human ghost.

The Púca is known to take on many forms, most often appearing as a dark horse, but also as an eagle, bat, bull, goat, a human man, or a more typical goblin-like small fairy; in the 1950 Hollywood movie 'Harvey' there is a Púca which is said to take the form of giant rabbit (Briggs, 1976; Yeats, 1888; McKillop, 1998). Which form or forms are attributed to the Púca are often dependent on what region the stories are coming from. In the form of a horse the Púca will lure riders onto its back and then take them on a wild ride, such as we see in this account:

"The people of the locality were scared of him and he was known as "Puca" .... He used not [to] be seen or heard by day, but by night if anyone passed through that field he would haul him on his back and begin to race all over the field with him. He used to run like the wind and if the man fell off his back he would haul him up again, before the man could have reached the ground. The field was not level but very hilly and the "puca" used to run as quickly up hill as downhill

One night a man passed through the field and the "puca" hauled him on his back and started to race all round the field, running into nooks and corners and out again. The man nearly died with fright and he started to roar. Once the "puca" raced faster than usual. "Oh Dia lem anam [oh God with my soul]" said the man. "Ah muse [ah me]" said the puca "tá baogal mór ort [you are in great danger]". The puca kept running until the man was nearly dead and after every mad fit of running the "puca" used to give a roar which could be heard all over the townland. When the man was nearly exhausted the "puca" threw him on the ground and disappeared."

(The Schools' Collection, Volume 0290, Pages 192- 194)

The Púca has also been known to work on farms and in mills, both in human form and in horse form (Briggs, 1976). He can be helpful when he chooses to and while he may torment some people there are also accounts of him being kind to travellers, particularly to people wandering home late at night and drunk. Although sometimes his kindness too is really mischief. In another account from the School's Collection we find a story of a Púca who encounters a piper with little talent for music who is going home late and drunk after a wedding. The Púca pulls the man up onto his back and demands he play for him, and when the man protests that he doesn't know the song the Púca wants to hear he is assured that the Púca will give him knowledge of how to play it. He then took the piper to the house of a Bean Sidhe on Croagh Patrick and had the man play for the gathered Otherworldly beings, again giving him the knowledge and skill to do so, and so well that he was rewarded with gold and a new set of pipes. However, when he was eventually returned home, he found that his skill to play was gone with the Púca and the gold had turned to withered leaves by the next morning. As his new set of pipes would only make the sound of geese he went to the priest, who wouldn't believe it until the man demonstrated, but when he put aside the new set and took up his old pipes, he found the skill the Púca had given him remained and he was known afterwards as the best musician in Mayo (The School's Collection, volume 0096, pages 292 – 297).

This, perhaps, best encapsulates the Púca's personality, using his shapeshifting and magic to both cause great fear and harm as well as minor mischief. Ultimately this being is mercurial and difficult to predict.

The Púca also had a special association with autumn and with the turning of the year form summer to winter. In some areas it was said that any berries which remained on the bushes after Michaelmas [29 September] belonged to the Púca, who would spoil them for human consumption (Briggs, 1976). In other areas it is said that it is after Samhain [31 October] that all the remaining berries belong to the Púca, and that he will urinate or spit on them to claim them. In either case it is clear that he was entitled to a portion of the wild harvest, the food that grew without being cultivated. The Púca was also associated more generally with roaming on and around Samhain and it was said that Samhain was sacred to him (Yeats, 1888).

Although generally helpful the Púca can play pranks which may be malicious and if it's necessary to convince one to leave a home or area, folklore would suggest the same method used (albeit less intentionally) that rids a place of a Grogach – the gift of clothes (Briggs, 1976; Yeats, 1888). In particular the gift of fine quality clothes as the Púca seems to have high standards. If, however, you feel you have a Púca around that you enjoy, you might try offering it the traditional cream or the less common offering of fish, as some say they enjoy that (Evans-Wentz, 1911).

Rónta

Seal Folk, more well-known in Scottish folklore under the name of selkies, in Irish folklore these beings are called Rónta (singular rón) literally meaning seals[9]; they may take human form on land or seal form in the water thanks to a magical seal skin which they can put on or off. They are sometimes also called mermaids in English although it should be understood these are not the traditional Mediterranean mermaids but a full bodied shapeshifter. Rather the term mermaid is applied to several distinct kinds of Irish beings as a sort of catch-all term that loses the nuances between them.

In this anecdotal account the seal woman is referred to in English as a mermaid, although she clearly fits the description of one of the seal folk using a seal skin to transform either in the sea or on land:

"There were mermaids also seen at it. They put seal skins around them. They came out of the water and took off the seal skin and danced on the bank. Anyone who got the skin could catch the mermaid. It is told a man caught the mermaid and married her. He hid the seal skin under the floor. She could not go back without the skin. She searched for the skin but could not get it. After about twenty years she got the skin and went back to the lake and she never was seen after."
(The School's Collection, vol 0229, p 427-428)

This pattern of a female Rón having her seal skin stolen and thus being forced into marriage with the human who has taken it is a common motif across folklore. The seal woman can't shapeshift to return to the sea without her seal skin and usually remains and has several children with the human man before either she finds the seal skin herself or one of her children finds it and shows it to her. Once she has the skin back, she immediately leaves.

Slua Sidhe

Slua Sidhe means fairy host or fairy assembly and represents a group of more malicious Otherworldly beings who travel through the air, often at night, and may waylay travellers. The Slua is most likely to be active at midnight and most often appears at night in general, but can show up at any time, sometimes startling farmers working in the fields (Evans Wentz, 1911). Anyone who had reason to be out at night, and more so if they were out alone, needed to be careful to avoid the fairy host.

The Slua Sidhe were known to force a human to go along with them while they engaged in their malicious endeavors, making the unlucky person aid them in their activities (O Súilleabháin, 1967). These endeavors often included kidnapping other people including brides, a common theme in many different types of fairy stories, and doing the new victim mischief. Anyone caught out alone, especially at night, or in a place they shouldn't be in could be swept up by the Slua with little choice but to go along with the Fairy Host until they were released. People taken this way might be said to be *"in the fairies"* (O Súilleabháin, 1967). In folklore and folk tales people taken by the Slua Sidhe could be taken and left far away, sometimes in foreign countries with no option but to find their way slowly home, or else may be returned to the place where they were taken mostly unharmed. The Slua is utterly capricious in how they treat those they take.

There are also tales of those who were out walking at night

and saw another person who had been or was being taken by the Slua, usually as the Slua was passing near the bystander. A folk method to get the Host to release anyone they may have taken is to throw the dust from the road, an iron knife, or similar object towards the Host which would be compelled to release the person they had taken. Those known to have been taken and released were gone to for advice relating to the fairies and seen as being quite knowledgeable about them, just as those who had more amicable relationships with the fairies were (O Súilleabháin, 1967).

The Slua Sidhe may include fairy horses, hounds, and a variety of fairy beings, as well as the human dead. Evans Wentz related stories of the Slua as both the mortal dead and as fallen angels, showing that the belief like other beliefs around the Good Folk, was not simple or straightforward (Evans Wentz, 1911). In Irish folktales related by authors like Yeats and Hyde, however, the fairy host are distinct from the human dead and act like fairies in other tales, engaging in behavior such as stealing human brides to force them to wed members of their own group.

The fairy host, like other fairies, is usually invisible to humans but can be sensed in the appearance of a sudden wind and the sound of voices, armor clinking, or people shouting (O Súilleabháin, 1967). Hyde describes it in the story 'Guleesh Na Guss Dhu' this way:

"he heard a great noise coming like the sound of many people running together, and talking, and laughing, and making sport, and the sound went by him like a whirl of wind..."
(Hyde, 1890, p 76).

Some say the Slua appears as a dust devil which moves over roads and hedges as the Good Neighbors travel (JCHAS, 2010). When the whirlwind appeared people would react by averting their eyes, turning their backs, and praying, or else saying "*Good luck to them, the ladies and gentlemen"* (O hOgain, 1995; JCHAS, 2010, p. 319). This of course reflects the common practice of appeasing the more dangerous fairies both by speaking of them in polite, positive terms and also of wishing them well, giving a blessing in hopes they respond in kind. This was done to avert any harm caused by the close proximity of the Host and to hopefully avoid drawing their attention in a negative way. The sí gaoithe [fairy wind] which indicated the Slua was present, could bring illness or cause injury as it passed by, contributing to its fearsome reputation (MacKillop, 1998).

End Notes

1. We do not recommend licking newts.

2. A keening woman was someone who would cry at a funeral, a sort of professional mourner.

3. In other dialects badb is pronounced bayv or bive.

4. Translation here is my own, and any errors are mine.

5. And subsequently should be taken with a large grain of salt.

6. Some of this material has been expanded and revised from my 'A New Dictionary of Fairies'

7. The borrowing of Latin terms into old and middle Irish is very common and can be found across the preserved language. This does not indicate that the concepts they are attached to are necessarily foreign to Irish culture only that the term we now have for them comes is etymologically from Latin. For example, one name for the owl, coileach oidhche [literally night hag], incorporates the word caillech, an older form of Cailleach, which is borrowed in from the Latin pallium, meaning veiled.

8. This was related to me by an older woman talking about her memories of childhood stories about fairies.

9. Both selkie and rón are words which mean seal and are used interchangeably for both regular seals and the magical seal folk.

Chapter 5

Safe Dealings

Throughout the recorded accounts of the Aos Sidhe there have always been humans who have encountered and interacted with these beings, sometimes with good results and sometimes with bad results. For those who find this subject interesting in a modern context it is worth understanding that these interactions, intentional or accidental, have their own set of rules at play. Ultimately there really is no guaranteed safety when this subject is at issue, but there are certainly ways that dealing with the Good Folk can be safer, and that is what we will be discussing here. We will cover proper etiquette for the Daoine Eile, offerings, and protections.

While it has become a bit of a trend to view the Good Folk as entirely benevolent and helpful even a brief look at the actual folklore and anecdotal accounts shows the real risks of encountering or dealing with these beings. Taking the safer approach is always the better choice and many people prefer to avoid the Good Folk altogether when possible.

Etiquette

The Good Folk are not human[1] and they do not operate by human rules or follow expected human behaviour, and to understand them you must understand that. They also seem to often have a double standard where humans are concerned, for example, they react very badly to humans stealing from them or damaging what belongs to them, yet they don't hesitate to steal from their human neighbours or cause great harm to humans who offend them. Below I will offer a rough list of basic etiquette around these beings as found throughout folklore and modern accounts.

Privacy – The Daoine Maithe are well-known for their dislike of being spied on or having their privacy invaded. Many stories in folklore involve a person who stumbles across the Good People engaging in an activity like hurling or dancing, is seen watching, and punished severely – in only a few cases does the person manage to talk their way out of any repercussions. In one such story a man saw a group of the Daoine Maithe playing a game of hurling in a field and called out to them at which they turned on him and beat him senseless. It is usually best not to acknowledge that you can see them unless it's clear they intended you to.

Silence – It is possible for a person to have the favor of the Other Crowd and to gain by it. However, they have a strict rule about a human not speaking of experiences or blessing they get from the Good People. Those who brag about fairy blessings or gifts almost always lose them and the future possibility of them. There are also cases, such as we see in the story of Lushmore, where a person talking about blessing from the Good People lead others to try to earn the same with disastrous results.

Proper Order – The Daoine Maithe are very invested in the proper order of things, not only in a household being clean and organized but in people following expectations. Humans who defy these expectations may be open to consequences. For example, there are several stories about a woman who stayed up late to continue spinning or weaving only to be interrupted by the Good Folk one way or another; the human being up after they should have gone to bed seems to allow the Good Folk to enter a place even if they normally could not. For example, in one story in The School's Collection a woman who stays up late is interrupted after midnight by a group of fairy hags who enter and tell her to fix them tea; they are only finally gotten rid of when she pretends the local hill, which is their home, is on fire[2] causing them to rush out and allowing her to bar the door against them (The Schools' Collection, Volume 0102, Page 276).

Food and Drink – The most well-known prohibition around food and the Good Folk is certainly the rule not to eat fairy food. The general belief is that to eat the food of the Othercrowd is to be irreversibly bound to them and their world (Ó hÓgáin, 1995). We see a wide range of anecdotes centered on this idea, usually featuring a human who has encountered a group of the Fair Folk and been invited or inveigled to join them, been offered food or drink, and is then cautioned by a human among the group (often recognized as a recently deceased community member) not to take the offered meal. The warning always includes the explicit message that if the food or drink is accepted the person will not be able to leave and return to the mortal world or their family.

However, while this is a firm rule with most of the Good Folk there is one notable exception, when the food is being offered by one of the Kings or Queens of the sidhe. We have various folkloric accounts of Finnbheara and Donn Fírinne inviting humans to join them for feasts and allowing them to leave afterwards with no ill effects. In that case it would be rude to refuse the food.

Hospitality – there is a standing expectation of hospitality and we find various stories where people suffer for denying such to the Good Folk or are rewarded for offering it. As with anything else with these beings, however, the issue is complex and there are also stories where hospitality puts the human in a bad position, such as when a group of fairies comes to a home late at night and refuses to leave. The general consensus seems to be that a degree of hospitality and welcome should be given to the Daoine Maithe but it is also wise to ward against them.

Don't lie to the Good People – The Good Folk seem to expect strict honesty from humans and tend to react badly in stories to finding out they have been lied to. They also seem to take anything they are told as truth, assuming the veracity of the words, which may be why in some stories they appear easy to trick with simple lies, such as the story related (in Irish) in the School's Collection where a woman trying to recover a man who has been taken by the Good People tells a fairy Queen she (the human) is the daughter of a king and demands a large gift from her; when the Queen can't produce all of it she is forced to return the stolen man (The Schools' Collection, Volume 0426, Page 559). Once they figure out that they have been lied to, they tend to retaliate.

Lending and Borrowing – It happens that the Good Neighbors do sometimes ask the loan of things from humans, and it usually wise to give it. This can range from food to give to a cow or milk (Ó Súilleabháin, 1967). They always repay their debts, most often with interest but not always in kind; for example, there is a well-known anecdote about a man who lent the Good Folk wheat and was repaid with more than he gave but in barley. Humans may also borrow from the Gentry but slightly more caution is required as folklore tells us that a deadline for re-payment is always set and must not be missed (MacNeill, 1962).

The Issue of Wash Water – This one is a bit complex, but generally speaking, one should not throw dirty water on the ground without an audible warning first, to alert any of the Good Folk who may be passing by, and one should not pour such water out over a large rock, lest it be the abode of the Daoine Maithe. They abhor filth and seem to have an especial hatred of dirty water and urine (both of which can be used as protection against them). There is also the matter of having dirty water standing in the home, something that was more common in the past when people would come in and wash their feet; this 'foot water' depending on the area of belief would either drive fairies away or conversely allow them entry into an otherwise protected home (Ó hÓgáin, 1995).

Offerings

There is a long tradition of giving the Daoine Maithe a portion of what we have, be that crops or milk or alcohol, with the belief that they are owed this portion as their due. This likely relates to the much older mythology that claims the first humans in Ireland made a deal with the Aos Sidhe – specifically via the Tuatha Dé Danann – to give them a tithe of their crops and milk in exchange for success in the land. While the idea may at its core be very old it has survived into relatively modern times, being referenced by Máire MacNeill in her book Festival of Lughnasa as a practice still found in the 20th century. She recounts the words of several farmers who believed that the fairies were owed a tenth of each harvest and would collect and store it, although as one source said *"The top pickle of all grain belongs to the Gintry; sometimes they claim it and sometimes not…"* (MacNeill, 1962, page 585). The top portion of all alcohol distilled, particularly outside distilleries, belongs to the Good People and was poured out as an offering to them.

This example was relayed to MacNeill by a man from Limerick, who was himself repeating something told him by a friend about a late 19th century Lughnasá gathering on Cnoc Fírinne:

"Fry-chawns³, flowers, and fruit were left for the unseen residents of the hill, ie Donn-Firine and his host as well as leprechauns and fairies. On that night these sidheoga [sióga] used to be seen frequently on the hill about that festival."
(MacNeill, 1962, p 205).

There is some debate today about whether it is proper to offer to the Good Folk and I think it's important to be clear that when we are talking about offerings, we mean either giving to them so that they won't cause harm or take things or giving to them because it is something that, in a technical sense, already belongs to them. My grandfather was in the habit of pouring out a bit of drink to the Good Folk and he always said it was because that bit was their due, and this seems to reflect a much older and wider belief. To give to them preserves a balance between the human community and the Daoine Eile.

Protections

Iron is usually viewed as a superlative defense against the Good People although exactly how the iron is used varies slightly. An iron horseshoe above the entrance to a home is a traditional protection which also is thought to draw luck to a home. Cold iron (iron weapons, especially bladed ones) are commonly recommended as its thought the Good Folk will flee from a bared iron blade. A black handled knife is thought to be particularly effective (Ó Súilleabháin, 1967).

Hazel has some protective qualities along with several other herbs, including Saint John's Wort and Mugwort. Rowan is also known to be a good protection against them, particularly when fashioned into a cross or circle. Folk accounts of people attempting to rescue those taken by the Daoine Maithe mention using a twig of rowan to break the enchantment holding the person (Foster, 1951). There are numerous charms to defend against these beings; in the Irish there are specialists called fairy doctors or bean feasa to help people afflicted by the Daoine Sidhe. Additionally salt has its protective uses and many of the Good Folk seem to be averse to Christian symbols and items.

As mentioned in Chapter 2, Samhain and to a lesser extent Bealtaine, are periods when the Good Folk are more active and because one is more likely to encounter these or other members of the Othercrowd during this time it is wise to carry extra protections with you, whether that's a bit of iron in your pocket or some rowan and red thread, or perhaps some holy water or a bit of salt. If you encounter the Slua Sidhe avert your eyes and to say something like *'good luck to them, the Ladies and Gentlemen'* so they will pass you by unmolested; if you think they may have a person with them or are trying to take someone near you, you can throw some dirt from the road, a glove, or knife in the air and yell *'this is yours that is mine'*. Should you encounter the Slua Sidhe hiding is always a safe option as its uncertain whether they will ignore you and pass by or choose you for some entertainment.

Bealtaine also has an array of particular protections associated with the increased risk of the time. Protections against harm from the Other Crowd included primrose and gorse scattered on the doorstep, and Rowan branches hung over the doorway (Evans, 1957). Yarrow was hung in the home to ward off illness, and a loop of ash might be used to protect a person against Themselves; it was also said looking through the loop would allow someone to see them even through the fairies' illusions (Evans, 1957; Danaher, 1972). Iron should be carried, ideally a black handled iron knife, or else ashes from the hearth fire, and if one is being misled or tormented by the Good People one could turn their jacket inside out to confuse them, or, in more dire circumstances, they could splash urine on their hands and face[4] (Danaher, 1972). Of course the most commonly used protection may simply be staying inside and avoiding any chance encounters.

The Good Folk across several cultures are well known for their preference for cleanliness and their strong dislike of people and places that are unclean as well as things, like urine and dirty water, that are similarly unclean. They avoid humans who they judge not to meet their cleanliness standards or may punish them and on the same side of that coin may be warded off by using the things they dislike. I'll include examples here for illustration.

Katherine Briggs, speaking generally about fairies in her 1976 'Dictionary of Fairies' mentions how dirty water left in a home might be punished by leg injuries or pinching. She also mentions that habitual uncleanness was a trait abhorred by the fairies and one which they frequently punished.

In some Irish folklore dirty wash water was a ward against fairies, keeping them out of a home (Ó hÓgáin, 1995). In other regions, however, the opposite effect resulted from not throwing dirty water out, as having it standing in the home allowed fairies to enter. There are several accounts of folklore around the need to call out a warning before throwing out or dumping dirty water, lest the Good Folk passing invisibly by be splashed by it and then seek to punish the person who had thrown it.

Urine, like dirty water, offended the fairies[5] and also acted to keep them away. As mentioned in Chapter 3 urine was used to drive off a changeling, and we have accounts such as that of Bridget Cleary, where the presumed changeling was doused in urine with the idea that it would cause the fairy to flee and force the return of the stolen human.

We have this from county Kerry, discussing the use of urine as a protection:

"To keep the fairies away from stealing or harming children the mothers washed them in urine and then the good people would not come near."
(The Schools' Collection, Volume 0464, Page 210)

And from Limerick a slightly longer story:

"Many years ago there was a woman living near Kilfinane and she had an only daughter who was very handsome. One morning when she was going to school she was passing through a field in which there was a lios [fairy fort]. When she was passing the lios a beautiful red haired woman stood in front of her and took her in to the lios to mind her child. And in the evening when the other children came home from school she left her go. The following morning the same thing happened and was going on for a number of days and the girl never told her mother about it but the mother noticed that her daughter was getting delicate. One day a neighbour came to her and asked her what was wrong with her daughter that she wasn't going to school. The mother said that her daughter left the house every morning to go to school, but she said that she noticed her getting

delicate and not eating her food like she used to. So she asked the little girl that night about not going to school and where was she spending the day and the little girl said "Don't blame me mother I was called by a lovely lady and she took me into her house to mind her baby for her and when the children used to be coming home from school she used to let me go." Her mother was very worried and did not know what to do. So she went to an old woman who was a neighbour of hers to get her advice. And the old woman told her to tell her daughter to ask the lady what cure was there for a pet calf that would be pining away. And the next morning the little girl asked the lady for the cure and she told her to tell her mother that the best cure was to wash it in urine for nine mornings, so when the little girl came home she told her mother what the red haired lady said. And the mother went and told the old woman about the cure. Then the old woman told the mother to bathe her daughter next morning in the urine. And she did. When the girl was passing the lios the next morning in her way to school she was met by the lady who told that she couldn't interfere with her anymore."

(The School's Collection, Volume 0510, Page 123).

An account from Donegal relates how a man set up a cowshed in a way that the urine from the cows flowed into the home of the local fairy queen, annoying her so that she killed and injured his cows. On the advice of an old woman, who the neighbours later decided was herself one of the Good People, he moved the cowshed and his luck turned around.

This is only a brief overview of some of the accounts of the Aos Sidhe being averse to dirty water and urine but hopefully it offers the reader a sense of the wider beliefs. The Good Folk are, as Briggs discusses at greater length, beings that prefer cleanliness and order and tend to react poorly to the opposite conditions even punishing those who they feel are slighting them or intentionally failing to offer them an appropriately clean place. This aversion can be used against them as shown in the stories about urine being used to protect children[6].

Final Thoughts

Ultimately there is no truly safe dealings with these beings and even people who specialize in this have their struggles sometimes. But there are some ways, as discussed here, to be slightly safer when around these beings or if you believe they are nearby.

End Notes

1. Even if some of them originally were human they collectively are not anymore.

2. This is a very common trope found in many such stories where a group of invading fairies is tricked out of a home by a human claiming their sidhe is on fire.

3. Fry-chawns or in Irish Fraocháns are a type of berry.

4. The Good People detest filth and things like dirty wash water and urine are known to disgust them, and so act as protections against them. We subsequently discuss this in more depth.

5. There are similar beliefs in Iceland, where the expression 'driving out the elves' is slang for urination, as it was believed that urinating offended the Álfar and would cause them to leave an area.

6. I'm not personally advocating bathing babies or children in urine. I am merely presenting it here as a folk belief to illustrate the Aos Sidhe's abhorrence of the substance and its power over them.

Chapter 6

Popular Misconceptions

As we wrap up this book, I would like to quickly address some of the more common misconceptions that I run across in relation to the Irish Aos Sidhe. Some of these are simple misunderstandings or conflations with outside folklore, but others are more problematic for various reasons.

In recent years there has been a notable increase in the popularity of fairies and particularly in the Daoine Sidhe or Sidhe. They are appearing across fiction and gaming as well as in various corners of paganism, however, the versions that find their way into many of these sources are far from the actual Irish sidhe. Popculture is filled with beings labelled as 'sidhe' who are in truth the creations of the people writing or talking about them rather the Otherworldly beings of Irish folklore. There has also been an increasing tendency to conflate the Irish sidhe with other beings across Celtic language cultural folklore, particularly the related but distinct Scottish Sìthe. My goal here is to untangle some of these modern confusions after having presented as much of the beliefs around the Aos Sidhe as possible in the text so far, so that people can understand the distinct threads of belief attached to them and appreciate the value that it has.

The Seelie and Unseelie Courts – Although gaining a great deal of ground thanks to modern fiction, the idea of the Seelie and Unseelie courts comes from Scottish, not Irish, folklore and isn't found in Irish folk belief. The terms Seelie and Unseelie are themselves from the Scots language and represent an understanding of the Good Neighbours that divided them into factions based on their benevolence or animosity towards humans. Irish belief doesn't have such a view, instead seeing all of the Good People as ambivalent at best and prone to both helping or harming. While there are some Irish Otherworldly beings who are more generally malicious, like the Each Uisce, they were never segregated into a specific grouping.

Who Rules the Irish Fair Folk? – In Irish folklore there are various Kings and Queens of particular sidhe. We know this from both mythology and more modern stories which attribute certain locations to named beings who are understood to be monarchs. In most cases these beings were once deities, members of the Tuatha Dé Danann, and are still thought to have a powerful influence over things around them. Unfortunately you will run across various sources in both fiction and non-fiction that attribute the rulership of Irish fairy hills or the Irish Otherworld more generally to outside beings like Oberon and Titania. This seems to be because of the popularity of those names but I would hope it goes without saying that putting English literary fairies in charge of Ireland's Otherworld is inappropriate. There is no shortage of named Irish Kings and Queens of the Otherworld so dragging in outside beings is unnecessary.

The Bean Tighe Fairy – This is a classic example of a source being misunderstood and twisted to create something entirely new and foreign to actual folk belief. Bean Tighe (modern Irish bean an tí) means woman of the house or housekeeper and has no supernatural associations. If you do a quick online search for 'Bean Tighe' you will turn up multiple links to articles and sites from the last decade all of which will describe a gentle friendly fairy, often referring to her as a type of Brownie house spirit, who cleans around a home and watches over children. Images of her, again found online, depict a plump grandmotherly figure. All emphasize her Irish folklore and many connect her to the witch hunt period, claiming that human women who had a Bean Tighe in their home would intentionally mess the house up a bit in the morning to hide the thoroughness of the Bean Tigh's cleaning lest other people notice and accuse them of witchcraft for having a fairy helper[1].

There was one reference to a fairy Bean Tighe in a 20th century source but that was far from the modern invention, however, since the modern one used the archaic spelling of the 20th century source, I felt safe in assuming that the modern idea was based, albeit very loosely, on that older one. We will begin then with the older source, which is a single paragraph in Evans-Wentz's 'Fairy Faith in Celtic Countries'.

The entire entry about the Bean Tighe in Evans-Wentz's book:

"The Bean-Tighe -The Bean-Tighe, the fairy housekeeper of the enchanted submerged castle of the Earl of Desmond, is supposed to appear sitting on an ancient earthen monument shaped like a great chair and hence called Suidheachan, the 'Housekeeper's Little Seat' [sic literally seat], on Knock Adoon (Hill of the Fort), which juts out into the Lough. The Bean-tighe, as I have heard an old peasant tell the tale, was once asleep on her Seat, when the Buachailleen, or 'Little Herd Boy' [sic little boy] stole her golden comb. When the Bean-Tighe awoke and saw what had happened, she cast a curse upon the cattle of the Buachailleen, and soon all of them were dead, and then the 'Little Herd Boy' himself died, but before his death he ordered the golden comb cast into the Lough."

Evans-Wentz also suggests in a footnote that the Bean-Tighe is elsewhere called the Bean Sidhe and identifies her with Áine. The story as related by Evans-Wentz is far more like a Bean Sidhe story than anything else, even featuring the golden comb, so I'm personally inclined to believe this probably was Bean Sidhe lore rather than a distinct being.

That all said it seems clear that the passage was not meant to refer to a fairy called a 'Bean-tighe' but to a fairy bean tighe, or fairy housekeeper. The name literally means 'woman of the house' or 'housekeeper' and is used in modern Irish with absolutely no fairy connotations. In the same way the Buachailleen mentioned wasn't the name of a type of fairy but simply a term in Irish that was being applied to a being in the story. To make either of these terms a fairy being the word sidhe (or sí) would have to be included, hence bean sidhe = fairy woman or cú sidhe = fairy hound; without including that it just means what it means, bean an tí, woman of the house. The fact that the author translates suidheachan (modern Irish suíochán) not as chair or seat but as 'housekeeper's little seat' makes me extremely skeptical that they had any Irish themselves; if they did, it shows they were being extremely loose and creative with their translations.

This is the sum total of the 1911 source and I am aware of no other references in books on Irish folklore or fairies of this until 2002. At this point Anna Franklin included the Bean Tighe in her 'Illustrated Encyclodaedia of Fairies', largely relying on Evans-Wentz's account but also adding that the Bean Tighe was an "*Irish House faerie*" who looked like a nice old woman and helped around a home in exchange for a bowl of cream. In 2006 a website and book 'Creatures of the Celtic Otherworld' by the author Andrew Paciorek shows up with an entry on the Bean Tighe. both Franklin and Paciorek used the same spelling as Evans-Wentz which is different from the modern Irish making it notable. Subsequent articles about this fairy would preserve the archaic spelling as well. Paciorek's Bean Tighe was different from the 1911 version, however, in almost every detail and made no mention of Evans-Wentz's account. Whereas Evans-Wentz's Bean-Tighe was like the Bean Sidhe found elsewhere, Paciorek's Bean Tighe was a cross between a Brownie and a live-in nanny. He described an exclusively female fairy that cleaned up houses at night, watched after children, and cared for pets; he compared her to a fairy godmother. He also claimed that during the witch hunts the Bean Tighe's work was so good that women would intentionally disrupt it lest they be thought to be witches trucking with spirits. He specifically mentions that the Bean Tighe loved strawberries with cream. All of these details would go on in the following decade and a half to be repeated and in some places added to; the repetition of key details again makes it easy to see that this is the root source even on articles that don't cite any references.

So, that is the actual history of the Bean Tighe such as I have found it. The fairy is decidedly not from Irish folklore – the first several authors writing about the Bean Tighe as a fairy were in England and offered no sources for their claims that this being was found in Irish folklore. Franklin's only clear source was Evans-Wentz who as we can see did not describe the fairy housekeeper's appearance and made no mention at all of her being helpful or even attached to human households; he said only that she was the housekeeper in a fairy "castle". The later details that have been added seem to blend existing folklore around Brownies with a more modern view of fairies in general and use little more than the name from Evans-Wentz's account.

Twee Winged Fairies – This one is more complicated as images of small winged fairies are becoming more popular across Ireland. I will simply point out here that this version of the Good Folk comes from the Victorian era, primarily English and American cultures, and that descriptions of these beings in Ireland prior to the late 20th and 21st century didn't include small, winged sprites that were helpful and granted wishes. Wings came into vogue through fiction via art and via the theater, probably (according to Dr Simon Young[2]) rooted originally in Paracelsus's writings on sylphs. When the Aos Sidhe fly in folkloric accounts it's either done with a type of magic or through the use of fairy horses which are actually enchanted ragweed.

The Aos Sidhe as Nature Spirits or Elementals – Another idea, or more accurately two joined ideas, that have been gaining a lot of ground recently are that the Aos Sidhe are either nature spirits or elementals, or sometimes both. While the idea of fairies in general as nature spirits has become very popular it's actually a fairly new idea, rooted in the late 19th century. Theosophy, beginning at this time, looked to the views of Paracelsus about elemental spirits and blended them with the Victorian romanticism of nature to give us the fairy as embodiment of and protector of the natural world. It is true if we look to Greek or Roman cultures that we can find beings like dryads and naiads who are spirits of specific natural features, but I would argue that the classical understanding of these beings is not the same as the modern concept of a nature spirit. In any event the Celtic language speaking cultures specifically do not seem to have any equivalent concept, with their Otherworldly spirits being territorial to specific places or things (wells, tress, rocks) but not as aspects or spirits literally of those things; in fact we have multiple stories across Ireland of the fairies moving their homes or leaving a place in a way that a nature spirit by definition could not do. This is important, not to dissuade people who choose to believe in nature spirits as fairies, or even of the Aos Sidhe as nature spirits, but so that everyone can have a wider context for these beings that is open to multiple options and aware of the history of specific beliefs.

The Aos Sidhe Are the Human Dead – This is of course partially true as we've mentioned previously there is folk belief that some human dead end up with the Aos Sidhe or are counted among their numbers. I'm increasingly seeing the nuance removed from the discussion though and people simply saying that all human dead become Aos sidhe or all Aos Sidhe were once human dead and that isn't true. Folk belief varies greatly on the subject and it's important not to reduce anything with these beings to simple answers.

The Good Folk are Vegetarians – This is a more modern idea that seems to be creeping in to belief and it may be true of some specific beings; however, there is a good amount of evidence across belief that the Good Folk can and do eat meat of various kinds. They are known to steal cows, drink milk, and to hunt and in various stories are described eating meat.

It is always best whenever you see anything claimed to be Irish folklore or fairy belief to double check it. There is sadly quite a lot of misinformation going around usually from people outside the culture or unfamiliar with the living beliefs who are either taking a creative approach or relying on bad sources themselves.

End Notes

1. Honestly this is so patently ridiculous I don't even know where to start debunking it. I'll just say that no self-respecting house wife or woman of the house would dirty a clean home because it was 'too clean', clean houses were not a sign that witch hunters looked for, and the witch hunts in Ireland were utterly different than elsewhere.

2. See his chapter 'When Did Fairies Get Wings?' in the 2019 book 'The Paranormal and Popular Culture' for an in-depth discussion of this.

Conclusion

"It is when we come to the fairies that we confront a belief which is perhaps as old as man himself, and which is still strong even in our own day..."
Seán Ó Súilleabháin, Nósanna agus Piseoga na nGael,
1967, page 82

It is often said that the Aos Sidhe are perpetually leaving but never gone and I have found this to be true, although mass media and the ease of the internet are unquestionably contributing to an increase in confusion around them and loss of the older beliefs. Nonetheless the Aos Sidhe continue to be an important aspect of folk belief and while many people today will deny believing in them few will deny their existence or the risk of offending them. To paraphrase more than one person asked if they believe in the Aos Sidhe: *'I don't believe in Them but they are there'*. They persist, as they always have, across time and across belief.

The beliefs around the Aos Sidhe are multilayered and diverse, and touch on every aspect of human life while also contradicting human expectations. They are beings who are known to indulge in human vices like smoking and alcohol but who also have strict standards of behaviour foreign to their human neighbors. They expect cleanliness and order but won't hesitate to cause difficulties, mess, and disorder when motivated to, or even when simply in the mood to. They seem by most accounts immortal and yet also worry over Christian salvation; they are described as both pagan gods and Christian angels. They are embodiments of contradiction yet follow clear predictable patterns. They expect their places to be treated with respect, and will punish any who interfere with them, yet they never hesitate to treat humans like playthings even to the point of stealing away any human they wish to. They cause irreversible harm to humans seemingly without any remorse. And yet despite all of this, despite the poc sidhe and fairy-shot and changelings, they are endlessly enchanting and intriguing to humans.

Stories of these beings have been woven into Ireland's very earth for well over a thousand years. They echo across that stretch of time and resonate still in modern minds and hearts. For all that the Good Folk are said to be diminished and fading and soon to be gone they remain. Always leaving but never gone.

This little book has offered a glimpse into the beliefs and some of the practices around the Aos Sidhe but this should be understood as an introduction, not a comprehensive work. This is a subject with richness and depth that is full of regional variations and local stories that could fill volumes ten times the size of this one and I cannot encourage people strongly enough to get out there and find those stories. Keep seeking these beings in folklore and myth, anecdotes and personal experiences, in the land and in dreams.

This book is a beginning, not an end.

Appendix A:

Terms and Pronunciation Guide

I am including a list of terms and names used in this book as well as related terms along with a rough pronunciation and meaning. I hope this will help readers who don't have any Irish. The pronunciations are my best effort to relay how the word sounds to me, and I must note that there are dialect variations and alternate pronunciations in many cases but I cannot cover them all here. A good resource is the pronunciation guide at Teanglann.ie which can be found here https://www.teanglann.ie/en/fuaim/

I cannot write or read IPA so my attempts at phonetic pronunciations here are literal. Hopefully they will all be self-explanatory although I will note that (ch) has a sound like the Scottish loch or German ich which I don't know any clear way to render in English.

An bunadh beag – ahn buhn-aw byuhg – the little people
An dream aerach – ahn dryahm air-a(ch) – the people of the air
An dream beag – ahn dryahm byuhg – the little people
An mhuintir bheag – ahn woon-cheer vyuhg – the little family
An slua aerach – ahn sloo-uh air-a(ch) – the host of the air
An slua bheatha – an sloo-uh va-ha – the living host
Aos Sidhe – ace shee – People of the fairy hills
Badb – Bive – name of a goddess also a term for a supernatural woman, witch, and crow
Bainne – bahnyuh – milk
Bean feasa – bahn fah-suh – wise woman
Bean Sidhe – bahn shee – fairy woman
Bean tighe – bahn tee – woman of the house, housekeeper

Bunadh beag na farraige – buhn-aw byuhg nuh far-ih-guh – little people of the sea

Bunadh na gcnoc – Buhn-aw nuh g-nuk people of the hills

Cailleach – Kall-yuck – name of a goddess, also means crone, hag, witch

Caite – cawt-cheh – elf-struck

Cuid na gcnoc – cuhdj nuh g-nuk – part of the hills

Daoine beaga – dee-nuh byuhg – little people

Daoine Eile – dee-nuh elluh – Other People/ Other Crowd

Daoine Maithe – dee-nuh ma-ha – Good People

Daoine Sidhe – dee-nuh shee – People of the fairy hills

Daoine Uaisle – dee-nuh oosh-luh – Noble People

Dobharchú – doh-wer-(ch)oo – water dog

Dream na gcnoc – dryahm nuh g-nuk – people of the hills

Emhain Abhlac – ew-ehn av-lak – place of apples

Fear sidhe – fahr shee – fairy man

Iarlais – eer-luh-sh – changeling

Leannán Sidhe – lawn-ahn shee – fairy lover

Lios – liss – a ring fort, also a term sometimes used for a fairy hill

Lucht na mbearád dearg – lockt nuh m-ah-rwad – people of the red caps

Maighdean Mhara – Mawjahn vara – sea maiden, mermaid

Murúch – mur-ook – mermaid

Na hUaisle – anh oosh-luh – the Gentry

Na hUaisle bheaga – nu hoosh-luh vyuhg – the little Gentry

Piseog – pish-ohg – charm, spell, also superstition

Rath – rah – a ring fort, also a term sometimes used for a fairy hill

Rón – roh-n – seal

Sidhe – shee – fairy hill or being within a fairy hill

Sidhe gaoithe – shee gwee-huh – fairy wind

Sióg – shee-owg – fairies

Slua bheatha na farraige – sloo-uh va-ha nuh far-ih-guh –

living host of the sea

Slua sidhe – sloo-uh shee – Fairy host

Slua sídhe an aeir – sloo-uh shee ahn air – fairy host of the air

Slua sídhe na spéire – sloo-uh shee nuh spare-eh – fairy host of the sky

Taibhse – tiev-shuh – ghost, spectre, phantom

Uaisle na gcnoc – oosh-luh nuh g-nuk – gentry of the hill

Appendix B:

Resources for Further Study

There is so much out there that's bad quality, fiction put out as folklore, or just plain wrong that I think it's especially important for people to know where the good sources are. Below I'll give all the people, books, and sites that I specifically consider trustworthy sources on this topic. I highly recommend digging further into these sources to see who they recommend to build a good sense of trustworthy sources on this topic.

People

Eddie Lenihan – a renowned storyteller and also the author of several books, Eddie Lenihan is a great resource for folklore about the Good Folk. His book 'Meeting the Othercrowd' in particular, as well as his YouTube channel and the various other interviews of his available on that site.

Lora O'Brien – has a series called 'folklore friday' as part of a wider YouTube channel which often features fairylore and stories of the Irish Othercrowd. Lora also offers several classes through the Irish Pagan School covering the subject and has recently published a book on the subject.

Dr. Jenny Butler – Dr. Butler has several videos on YouTube discussing the Good People, and also offers a class through University College Cork called 'Myth and Magic an Introduction to the Study of Irish Folklore and Mythology' which discusses vital aspects of the Good Folk and the Otherworld.

Michael Fortune – a great resource for Irish folklore, including stories of the Othercrowd. He has a series of YouTube interviews he's done with people around Ireland discussing folklore, beliefs, and practices which includes a series of first and secondhand accounts of people interacting with the Daoine Maithe.

Hog and Dice – on both YouTube and TikTok, a great resource for Irish folklore and retelling of traditional stories.

The Crafty Cailleach – videos can be found on YouTube and TikTok discussing Irish culture and folklore. Of particular interest will be the video 'Five Fundamentals of the Irish Fair Folk – Irish 'Fairy' Basics'.

Books

'The Banshee' by Patricia Lysaght – the author's dissertation, this book is literally everything you could ever want to know about the Bean sidhe.

'Meeting the Othercrowd' by Lenihan and Green – mentioned above this book is a collection of stories about the Good Folk.

'The Fairy Faith in Ireland: History, Tradition, and Modern Pagan Practice' by Lora O'Brien – a wide ranging look at fairy beliefs in Ireland, including personal anecdotes and older folklore, along with practical modern guidelines.

'Tales of the Wicklow Hills' by Richard Marsh – a collection of stories and legends, as well as anecdotal accounts, from the Wicklow area. Includes accounts of púcaí, fairy trees, and fairy forts.

'Away With the Fairies' by William Henry – A collection of folktales and folk beliefs from Galway, including various stories of na Uaisle.

Websites

Ireland's Folklore and Traditions – excellent blog about traditional Irish beliefs, traditions, and folklore, with a great article about the 'reality of Irish fairies'.

Blúiríní Béaloidis – a podcast about Irish folklore with some excellent discussions of the Good People.

Circle Stories – a Facebook page that features articles discussing Irish folk beliefs, with many great articles about the Othercrowd and Otherworld.

Dúchas.ie – a treasure trove of folklore recorded in the early 20th century including many very important stories about the Daoine Maithe.

Fiction

I am often rather harsh about fictional depictions of these beings but there are several books that deal with the Irish Good People in a creative way that I do like and which I feel stays true to their nature as depicted in folklore. I'm going to include them here as well to wrap up this section.

Ruth Frances Long – this author has several series, but I especially want to highlight the Dubh Linn series which begins with 'A Crack in Everything'. It heavily involves the Good Folk, as well as a blend of other folklore and belief.

Peadar Ó'Guilín – this author has a two-book series 'The Grey Lands' which looks at an alternate world Ireland which has been cut off from the rest of the globe and is at the mercy of the Othercrowd.

Bibliography

Allingham, W., (1888) The Lepracaun; or Fairy shoemaker http://www.sacred-texts.com/neu/yeats/fip/fip24.htm

Briggs, K., (1976) A Dictionary of Fairies

--- (1978) The Vanishing People: Fairy Lore and Legends

Broderick, S., (2016) The Darker Side of Folklore: The story of Bridget Cleary. Retrieved from https://irishfolklore. wordpress.com/2016/12/18/first-blog-post/?fbclid=IwAR2 uWmr6dwzflJ803RKSst3AsmgHLbZvm60BcMZq0YyyCA iSlupTsC-UuKc

Carmichael Watson, J., (1941) Mesca Ulad. Retrieved from https://celt.ucc.ie/published/G301040.html?fbclid=IwAR 2FMdWZA3iyXUhcbb0h-uQWnlYsQkn0UggfStZD8o2o_ ZgpBK0D_HhAgUc

Colton, S., (2016) Take on Nature: Ireland's Only Newt a Real Mankeeper; The Irish News retrieved from https://www. irishnews.com/lifestyle/2016/04/09/news/take-on-nature- ireland-s-only-newt-a-real-mankeeper-474743/

Coulter, P., (2015) Fairy Tales: finding Fairy Bushes Across Northern Ireland. Retrieved from https://www.bbc.com/ news/uk-northern-ireland-31459851

Croker, T., (1825). Fairy Legends and Traditions http://www. sacred-texts.com/neu/celt/flat/index.htm

Daimler, M., (2015) Translating De Gabail in t-Sida. Retrieved from https://lairbhan.blogspot.com/2015/04/translating- de-gabail-in-tsida.html

--- (2017) Translating the Echtra Condla. Retrieved from https://lairbhan.blogspot.com/2017/03/ectra-condla- chaim-meic-cuind.html

--- (2021) Man Recovered from the Fairies – A story. Retrieved from https://lairbhan.blogspot.com/2021/02/ man-recovered-from-fairies-story.html

Danaher, K., (1972) The Year in Ireland

Dobs, M., (1929) Fosterage of the Two Milk Pails. Retrieved from http://www.maryjones.us/ctexts/fosterage.html

---- (1929) Zeitschrift fur Celtische Philologie vol 18

Echtra Fergusa Maic Leiti (n.d.) University College Cork. Retrieved from http://iso.ucc.ie/Echtra-fergusa/Echtra-fergusa-text.html

eDIL (2021) Electronic Dictionary of the Irish Language Retrieved from http://edil

Evans, E., (1957). Irish Folk Ways

Evans-Wentz, W. Y. (1966, 1990) The Fairy-Faith in Celtic Countries

Fortune, M., (2021) Folklore Collections. http://www. michaelfortune.ie/Folklore_Collection_Work.html

Foster, J., (1951) Ulster Folklore

Gregory, A., (1920) Visions & Beliefs in the West of Ireland

Harper, D., (2017) Online Etymology Dictionary: Leprechaun

Henry, W., (2020) Away With the Fairies

Hyde, D., (1890) Beside the Fire: A collection of Irish Gaelic Folk Stories

JCHAS (2010) Journal of the Cork Historical and Archaeological Society

Jenkins, R., (1991) *'Witches and Fairies: supernatural aggression and deviance among the Irish peasantry'*, The Good People

Lenihan, E., and Green, C., (2004) Meeting the Other Crowd

Lysaght, P., (1986) The Banshee

--- (1991) 'Fairylore from the Midlands of Ireland'; the Good People New Fairylore Essays

Marsh, R., (2007) Tales of the Wicklow Hills

MacCoitir, N., (2003) Irish Trees

MacNeill, M., (1962) The Festival of Lughnasa

McKillop, J., (1998) Dictionary of Celtic Mythology

Purkiss, D., (2000) At the Bottom of the Garden

Ó Crualaoich, G., (2003) The Book of the Cailleach: Stories of the Wise Woman Healer

Ó Dónaill, (1977) Foclóir Gaeilge-Béarla

O hOgain, D., (1995) Irish Superstitions

Ó Súilleabháin, S., (1967). Nósanna agus Piseoga na nGael

Reiti, B., (1991) 'The Blast' in Newfoundland Fairy Tradition'; The Good People

The School's Collection (2021) Dúchas National Folklore Collection, UCD Retrieved from https://www.duchas.ie/en/cbes

--- (2021) Béaloideas Volume 0426, Page 559. Retrieved from https://www.duchas.ie/en/cbes/4678409/4678231

--- (2021) Bean Sidhe Volume 0568, page 298. Retrieved from https://www.duchas.ie/en/cbes/4922256/4864629/5051963

--- (2021) Changelings Volume 0888, page 211. Retrieved from https://www.duchas.ie/en/src?q=changeling

--- (2021) Changeling Volume 0721, page 072. Retrieved from https://www.duchas.ie/en/cbes/5009029/4978998

--- (2021) Cu Sidhe The Schools' Collection, Volume 0010, Page 003. Retrieved from https://www.duchas.ie/en/cbes/4591079/4588451

--- (2021) Each Uisce Volume 1047, Page 24 Retrieved from https://www.duchas.ie/en/cbes/4428328/4395757/4461303

--- (2021) Fairies Volume 0102, Page 276. Retrieved from https://www.duchas.ie/en/cbes/4427867/4352052

--- (2021) Geancanach Volume 0491, Page 304 Retrieved from https://www.duchas.ie/en/cbes/4921975/4914662

--- (2021) Geancanach Volume 0978, Page 124 Retrieved from https://www.duchas.ie/en/cbes/5044838/5043050/5093655

--- (2021) Mermaids Volume 0491, Page 304. Retrieved from https://www.duchas.ie/en/cbes/4921975/4914662

--- (2021) Puca, Volume 0290, pages 192 – 194. Retrieved from https://www.duchas.ie/en/cbes/4921602/4883824

--- (2021) Puca, Volume 0096, pages 292 – 296. Retrieved from https://www.duchas.ie/en/cbes/4427839/4349075

--- (2021) Seals, Volume 0229, pages 427 – 428. Retrieved from https://www.duchas.ie/en/cbes/4658465/4658387

--- (2021) Urine Volume 0464, Page 210. Retrieved from https://www.duchas.ie/ga/cbes/4742085/4734431/4923997

--- (2021) Urine Volume 0510, Page 123 Retrieved from https://www.duchas.ie/en/cbes/4922044/4846951

--- (2021) Water horses, Volume 0380, Page 356 -357 Retrieved from https://www.duchas.ie/en/cbe/9000834/7183566

Wedin, W., (1998) The Sidhe, the Tuatha de Danaan, and the Fairies in Yeats's Early Works; William Butler Yeats Seminar

Wilde, E., (1888) Irish Cures, Mystic Charms & Superstitions

Williams, N., (1991) Semantics of the Word Fairy

Yeats, W., (1888) Fairy and Folktales of the Irish Peasantry

--- (1962) Celtic Twilight

Young, S., (2011) Changelings and the Law Retrieved from http://www.strangehistory.net/2011/08/11/changelings-and-the-law/

--- (2019) 'When Did Fairies Get Wings?', The Paranormal and Popular Culture

Other Fairy Titles by Morgan Daimler

A New Dictionary of Fairies
*A 21st Century Exploration of Celtic and Related
Western European Fairies*
978-1-78904-036-4 (paperback)
978-1-78904-037-1 (ebook)

Fairies
A Guide to the Celtic Fair Folk
978-1-78279-650-3 (paperback)
978-1-78279-696-1 (ebook)

Fairycraft
Following the Path of Fairy Witchcraft
978-1-78535-051-1 (paperback)
978-1-78535-052-8 (ebook)

Fairy Queens
Meeting the Queens of the Otherworld
978-1-78535-833-3 (paperback)
978-1-78535-842-5 (ebook)

Fairy Witchcraft
A Neopagan's Guide to the Celtic Fairy Faith
978-1-78279-343-4 (paperback)
978-1-78279-344-1 (ebook)

Living Fairy
Fairy Witchcraft and Star Worship
978-1-78904-539-0 (paperback)
978-1-78904-540-6 (ebook)

Other Irish Titles by Morgan Daimler

Brigid
Meeting the Celtic Goddess of Poetry, Forge,
and Healing Well
978-1-78535-320-8 (Paperback)
978-1-78535-321-5 (ebook)

The Dagda
Meeting the Good God of Ireland
978-1-78535-640-7 (Paperback)
978-1-78535-641-4 (ebook)

Manannán mac Lir
Meeting the Celtic God of Wave and Wonder
978-1-78535-810-4 (Paperback)
978-1-78535-811-1 (ebook)

The Morrigan
Meeting the Great Queens
978-1-78279-833-0 (Paperback)
978-1-78279-834-7 (ebook)

Raven Goddess
Going Deeper with the Morrigan
978-1-78904-486-7 (Paperback)
978-1-78904-487-4 (ebook)

Irish Paganism
Reconstructing Irish Polytheism
978-1-78535-145-7 (Paperback)
978-1-78535-146-4 (ebook)

MOON
BOOKS

PAGANISM & SHAMANISM

What is Paganism? A religion, a spirituality, an alternative belief system, nature worship? You can find support for all these definitions (and many more) in dictionaries, encyclopaedias, and text books of religion, but subscribe to any one and the truth will evade you. Above all Paganism is a creative pursuit, an encounter with reality, an exploration of meaning and an expression of the soul. Druids, Heathens, Wiccans and others, all contribute their insights and literary riches to the Pagan tradition. Moon Books invites you to begin or to deepen your own encounter, right here, right now.

If you have enjoyed this book, why not tell other readers by posting a review on your preferred book site.

Recent bestsellers from Moon Books are:

Journey to the Dark Goddess
How to Return to Your Soul
Jane Meredith
Discover the powerful secrets of the Dark Goddess and
transform your depression, grief and pain into healing
and integration.
Paperback: 978-1-84694-677-6 ebook: 978-1-78099-223-5

Shamanic Reiki
Expanded Ways of Working with Universal Life Force Energy
Llyn Roberts, Robert Levy
Shamanism and Reiki are each powerful ways of healing; together,
their power multiplies. *Shamanic Reiki* introduces techniques to
help healers and Reiki practitioners tap ancient healing wisdom.
Paperback: 978-1-84694-037-8 ebook: 978-1-84694-650-9

Pagan Portals – The Awen Alone
Walking the Path of the Solitary Druid
Joanna van der Hoeven
An introductory guide for the solitary Druid, *The Awen Alone* will
accompany you as you explore, and seek out your own place
within the natural world.
Paperback: 978-1-78279-547-6 ebook: 978-1-78279-546-9

A Kitchen Witch's World of Magical Herbs & Plants
Rachel Patterson
A journey into the magical world of herbs and plants, filled with
magical uses, folklore, history and practical magic. By popular
writer, blogger and kitchen witch, Tansy Firedragon.
Paperback: 978-1-78279-621-3 ebook: 978-1-78279-620-6

Naming the Goddess

Trevor Greenfield

Naming the Goddess is written by over eighty adherents and scholars of Goddess and Goddess Spirituality.

Paperback: 978-1-78279-476-9 ebook: 978-1-78279-475-2

Shapeshifting into Higher Consciousness

Heal and Transform Yourself and Our World with Ancient Shamanic and Modern Methods

Llyn Roberts

Ancient and modern methods that you can use every day to transform yourself and make a positive difference in the world.

Paperback: 978-1-84694-843-5 ebook: 978-1-84694-844-2

Readers of ebooks can buy or view any of these bestsellers by clicking on the live link in the title. Most titles are published in paperback and as an ebook. Paperbacks are available in traditional bookshops. Both print and ebook formats are available online.

Find more titles and sign up to our readers' newsletter at
http://www.johnhuntpublishing.com/paganism
Follow us on Facebook at https://www.facebook.com/MoonBooks
and Twitter at https://twitter.com/MoonBooksJHP